NICK OWEN

In the Time of Nick

NICK OWEN

In the Time of Nick

FOREWORD BY GREG DYKE

BREWIN BOOKS

First published by
Brewin Books Ltd, 56 Alcester Road,
Studley, Warwickshire B80 7LG in 2004
www.brewinbooks.com

ISBN 1 85858 257 1

A Cataloguing in Publication Record
for this title is available from the British Library.

Typeset in New Baskerville
Printed in Great Britain by
Cromwell Press

CONTENTS

ACKNOWLEDGEMENTS

I would like to mention a few people who have helped jog my rather inconsistent memory! They include Maurice Blisson, Stephanie Haponski, Howard Dartnall, Steve Minchin, John Payne, Jason Pollock, Kim Robson, John D. Taylor, Trish Williamson, Wincey Willis and Ian White. Wincey also allowed me to use some of her photographs, as has the BBC. Thank you all very much. Thanks also to Jill, Andy, Tim, Chris and Jenny for leaving me in peace on the computer to write this!

FOREWORD

by Greg Dyke

It is now more than twenty years since I first met Nick Owen. While some of us have visibly changed, Nick looks exactly the same as the fresh-faced, young sports reporter I met at TVam in 1983. For both us those were exciting times. Nick was promoted over the top of the "Famous Five" – the presenters who had together helped to win the breakfast franchise – to be the new face of TVam. I, after just five years working in television, had been given the job of Editor in Chief at TVam. We both had the same task – to save the ailing station which had few viewers, little advertising and was heading into bankruptcy. Together we lived through the funniest, most bizarre year of our lives. But whatever we did worked. In twelve months the station was turned around and as a result, with his long-term television partner Anne Diamond by his side, Nick literally became famous overnight.

Nick became a celebrity because he was a nice guy or "Mr Ordinary" as some in the press described him. He was, and is, as nice a guy as you will find in television; a straight guy, a family man, a man devoted to Luton Town Football Club – I suppose someone has to be. To this day he is still unflappable in front of camera and his great strength on television is that what you see is what he is, there's no side to him. The viewers like that about Nick and it's why he has been such a success over several decades.

I worked with Nick again when I was Chairman of ITV Sport in the late eighties and he was our number one sports presenter and again ten years later when I was Director General of the BBC and Nick presented BBC Midlands Today, our regional news programme for the West Midlands. He hadn't changed. A great television professional and a great bloke.

Greg Dyke

Picture previous page:
Nick Owen, John Stapleton and Greg Dyke.

PROLOGUE

He's in his twenties now, but son Tim was celebrating his second birthday with hordes of fellow toddlers and their mums, when I sneaked out of the party to head back to London from our Birmingham home for another sports shift at TVam. As I left, I said to my wife, Jill, "This could be the most important week in my working life."

The new breakfast station had been on air a mere eight weeks and ratings were dismally low. Sometimes, as few as four hundred thousand were watching and the whole company's future lay in grave doubt. As co-founder, David Frost, remarked at the time, "Working at TVam is like being on the Titanic – only the Titanic had entertainment."

David himself, it was rumoured, could be for the chop from presenting and there was gossip around the place that I would be asked to take over, at least for a while. All I did know at that stage was that Jonathan Aitken MP, then running the station after the resignation of Peter Jay, had been seeking me out over the last couple of days only to be told I was having a little time off.

At 8.15 on the morning of my return, after I had presented my sports bulletins, Jonathan called me into his office and, with a wry smile, uttered those immortal words, "I'm going to make you a star!"

Well, Jonathan, two decades on, I am still waiting, but thanks! He wanted to pitch me in from the following Tuesday after the Easter holiday. I climbed back onto my chair, accepted the offer and prepared for a month's trial alongside Angela Rippon and Anna Ford.

I honestly felt I could do the job, but following a man of David Frost's stature was daunting to say the least. I still wonder at Jonathan's guts in thrusting an unknown into the spotlight, so soon after the station's launch amid Hollywood style razmatazz. Jonathan must have wondered himself when a national magazine described me as an unknown, uncharismatic, unsexy, anonymous sports reporter from the Midlands!

I was told by Jonathan to say nothing in public at this stage, but that was never easy when the story of TVam was rapidly becoming a true-life soap opera. We were on the front pages nearly every day. I'll never forget bumping into an old colleague from the newsroom at Central TV, Tony Maycock. He shocked me with his scathing criticism of my decision to move to TVam and the potentially dicey waters of breakfast television, then, of course, in its infancy.

"Your audience is barely the size of a weekly newspaper," he said. "You must have been mad!"

At a time of deep concern for the future, it was hardly the comment you needed from a former workmate, but it shows you how tenuous things were at the time. I couldn't tell him I was about to replace David Frost either, not that it was seen as a panacea, more a holding operation until they could get a big name in.

Speculation still spread though, and my wife and I were staggered at the cars queuing up outside our house, with reporters desperately trying to get me to admit I was taking over. One guy I had been playing squash with a week earlier had a complete quote he'd made up for me to say, but I wouldn't agree to it. He still ran it in a national newspaper the next day!

The official announcement at a press conference on Easter Monday was attended by the man who was due to join us later in the month as our new editor-in-chief, Greg Dyke. We were going to be working together many times in ensuing years.

I became known as Mr. Ordinary because I described myself as an ordinary guy in comparison with the glamorous image of the so-called Famous Five, Anna, Angela, Michael Parkinson, Robert Kee and David. I hoped I would be easier to relate to for the average man and woman watching.

It was a strange sensation to be pictured on most of the front pages, to be on the other side of the journalistic fence, but it certainly beat covering council meetings with the Doncaster Evening Post where I started. Despite the hovering uncertainty, despite the constant digs in the press about individuals or the company as a whole, I was certain we would survive. We just needed time.

Greg revitalised the place. He changed the whole philosophy, we were gripped by his enthusiasm and ultimately TVam became one of the most successful television stations in the world.

So much happened to me in those three and a half years at TVam and beyond. We easily won the ratings war with the BBC, I had an extremely happy partnership with Anne Diamond, returned to ITV Sport and anchored the Olympics and football world cup, hosted three game shows, interviewed prime ministers and showbiz celebrities, had a female co-presenter who refused to speak to me, was very publicly sacked twice, crossed the globe for sporting events or travel shows, made some terrific friends and have somehow been a Dad to my four children. Let me tell you more.

Nick Owen and Midlands Today co-presenter Suzanne Virdee at The Mailbox, Birmingham, the BBC's new Midland headquarters.

Chapter One

THE BELLS, THE BELLS

I suppose it was inevitable that I would end up as a journalist. Even as a youngster, I was obsessed with news. I read the newspapers avidly from the age of seven and, at school, I created a handwritten, extremely unglossy magazine, mostly filled with sports news and opinion, when I was about 12 years old. I even organised a table tennis tournament, so that I could write about it. I also had a joke published in the Tiger comic around that time. I got ten shillings plus a letter from the Chief Chuckler, though I am slightly ashamed to admit I nicked it from the Rover! My parents also tell me I used to storm around our house commentating about imaginary goals into a soup spoon! Mind you, they and I could never have imagined then that I would commentate on the World Cup in Spain in 1982 and anchor the tournament for ITV in 1990. But that's getting ahead of ourselves.

I grew up in Berkhamsted, a small town in Hertfordshire, noted by train passengers for the ruined Norman castle close to the railway line on the approaches to London. It's only yards too from the Grand Union Canal and I always thought how intelligent it was of William the Conqueror and his boys to build the castle so near to such strategic points of travel. Some of my happiest memories and friendships stem from my childhood in Berkhamsted, with my particular mates Ian Phillips and Mike Tanner. We spent many hours together playing sport, making early forays with the opposite sex, frequenting some fabulous pubs and travelling hundreds of miles following our beloved Luton Town Football Club. My father, Bertie, was an esteemed headmaster in the town and my mother, Esme, taught music. A pleasant community in marvellous countryside amongst the Chilterns, very much my spiritual home.

What I found difficult was leaving it all three times a year to head off to boarding school. I went to Kingsland Grange prep school in

Shrewsbury at the age of seven, and on to Shrewsbury School, when I was 13. Both fine schools, but I didn't distinguish myself especially. One particular memory from my A level year makes me smile, though. I was caught by a teacher in the table tennis hut in a position of extreme friendship with a young lady on the domestic staff. My main punishment was having to write out a translation of the whole of Virgil's Aeneid Book Six. That came in very useful when it was my son Chris's Latin set book for GCSE nearly forty years later!

I went to Shrewsbury for my schooling because that's where my father went. He was a Shropshire lad and, as a teacher himself, understandably didn't fancy having me in his own school! Shrewsbury seemed a very long way from home in those days before the M1 was built. The journey by car was tortuous, so I travelled by train more often than not. Railway stations still give me the creeps! But one greater hangover, incredibly, is church bells. Sundays away from home were always somehow the worst, when I was very young. Boys who lived comparatively near the school would be picked up by their parents and race home for blessed respite from the rigours of 1950s boarding school. I was sometimes lucky enough to be invited along too and I still greatly appreciate the kindness of two families in particular, the Coxes and the Whittakers. But church bells still, even now, put me on a downer because of the association with those early days away from home. I hate them and even had them banned at my wedding!

I didn't enjoy the food much. I know the memory can play tricks, but our diet seemed to be dominated by beetroot and corned beef! I remember desperately trying to eke out the meagre supplies of butter in the morning – the rest of the time we made do with an amorphous blob of revolting margarine. We were not allowed our own supplies of tuck and I recall a friend being beaten when he was caught more than once with contraband sweets. I do, though, remember a gastronomic highlight. One morning in midwinter, the teachers left a load of porridge over and a friend and I scoffed the lot after everyone had gone. I can still see myself standing at the door of our dormitory saying, "Isn't it great to feel full for a change?"

I stole my first kiss when I was twelve. My friend Robin had built up a relationship with one of the girls on the residential cleaning staff. She was only sixteen, but she seemed really grown up to us. He used to sneak through the changing rooms to where the girls used to relax in the evenings and she would come out to meet him. Robin was quite mature for his age... I was still a little boy. He took me along to one of his assignations and promised I would get a kiss. Wow, was my heart beating! I can see him now with one last piece of advice which has stood me in good stead evermore...he advised me in the strongest terms to turn my face slightly, going in for the big moment, to avoid a clash of noses!

It was about that time I acquired my first pop record. Dynamite and Travelling Light by Cliff Richard. He was Britain's answer to Elvis, of course, but my folks didn't approve. They wouldn't even let me see his early films or Elvis's, for that matter. But, even before I had my own record player, I secured my first disc in a deal with a friend. I lent him my radio in return for Cliff's number one and I still have that single to this day. The friend, incidentally, went on to become the longest serving regional TV presenter in the Midlands, Bob Warman, over on ITV.

In these days of mobiles, it's hard to imagine that I never once phoned home in my first four years away at prep school. I used to write religiously once a week and that was checked by a duty master for spelling, punctuation and definitely content. But one day, someone told me how you could reverse the charges from a telephone box and talk to someone without paying. Groundbreaking! It intrigued me and, when I was spending a Sunday with a friend whose parents owned a hotel at Prees Heath, near Shrewsbury, I spotted my chance. I saw this phone box by a roundabout and called the operator. Quite a procedure, it seemed, to get through via trunks. Hello, Luton, hello Hemel Hempstead, hello just about every blooming town between Shropshire and Hertfordshire, and finally hello Berkhamsted, hello, will you take a call from Master Nicky Owen, and, hey presto, I was talking to my mother and she nearly fell off her legs!

I love my cricket, but it could have been so different after one agonising experience which scarred me for life and had frightening repercussions more than forty years later. I was playing cricket in short trousers when I chased a ball over the boundary and into the undergrowth. Before I knew it, I had passed through a wasps' nest and the little blighters rose up in fury. I was stung all over. About ten stings on my legs and one I will never, ever forget in the region of man's most treasured possession. God, it hurt! I ran screaming round the field before hurtling into the house to find matron. As a comparative youngster herself, probably early twenties, she must have been overwhelmed with embarrassment as I thrust my damaged goods in her face. Naturally, I asked her to remove the pain and keep the swelling! I was the biggest boy in the school for a week and had to withdraw from the final of the hundred yards on School Sports Day because I could hardly run! I will tell you about the knock-on effect later.

Overall, I have some fond memories of Kingsland Grange, particularly on the football and cricket field, and I was honoured to speak at the school's centenary dinner not so long ago. Reminiscences that night of a terrifying headmaster called Mac, who delighted in throwing an extremely hard, wood-backed blackboard cleaner at boys who had displeased him. He hurled it once in my direction, I ducked and it shattered the window behind. Then there was the fearsome old matron, Mrs. Olive Ruth. A dreadful woman, who I can still vividly see punching a small boy in the back with her fist. As my friend Bob Warman observed at the dinner, the only difference between Mrs. Ruth and a rottweiler was lipstick.

Something I am not particularly proud of during my time at the school must be one of the earliest recorded cases of football hooliganism. A slightly younger, but bigger, boy called Patrick insulted Luton Town F.C. and their captain, Syd Owen, no relation, after he had been voted Footballer of the Year for 1959. I tore into him in the bushes and thumped him so hard I had to write and apologise to his parents. His uniform was ripped to pieces and my mother and father had to stump up the money to replace it.

I went on to Shrewsbury School - one of the country's finest public schools - and still remember the shock of being surrounded by shaving six footers, when I was a skinny shrimp at four foot nine and a half! Centre stage in the amateur dramatics and my first house captain of football was Michael Palin. What a hero he was, even then! After one crucial house football match, he said about me in the house football annals, "Owen on the wing made up for his size with guts and enthusiasm."

Besides Palin, the school has produced a number of notable celebrities, many of them associated with the media and showbiz. Richard Ingrams and Willie Rushton of Private Eye fame went there, as too did the sixties phenomenon, Simon Dee, the first voice on pirate radio, who later enjoyed a brief spell as a highly-paid and highly-visible TV presenter. John Peel was in my house before my time, while his younger brother, Alan, was a close friend whom I still see today. Tory grandee Michael Heseltine went to Shrewsbury School, as did the comedian and broadcaster Nick Hancock.

And to complete the mixed bag, a close friend of mine for a spell was Roddy Llewellyn. Imagine my surprise years later when he hit the headlines as the paramour of Princess Margaret! We met up again for the first time in about twenty years when he became a regular contributor to the breakfast station, TVam. By that time, he and the Princess were just a memory and the gossip columnist, Nigel Dempster, was moved to say one day on the show, "All that's under Princess Margaret's duvet these days is dust!"

I have mentioned my innocent escapades with Robin and a sixteen year old girl who worked at Kingsland Grange prep school, but my first real, nearly grown-up, full-on kiss happened in Berkhamsted with a lovely girl called Philippa. She was 5ft 5 and I was 5ft 3, so the best action was usually to be had sitting down and, boy, do I remember that first smacker in the back row of the Rex Cinema. We were watching the Elvis Presley film, Kid Galahad. My friend Paul was far more progressive than I was and had a grip on his companion within minutes of the opening titles. I was pathetically backward, but he egged me on mercilessly until I took the plunge sometime during Elvis's third number. It was positively electric, like being plugged into the national grid. That knee-trembling moment remains a very special memory.

I left school in the summer of '66, when England gloriously won the World Cup on a baking summer's day and my father, a huge football fan all his life, missed it because he was at a wedding! Luckily, the reception was only yards from our house, so he kept nipping in to catch up with the score and report back to his fellow guests. Our living room was packed with friends of mine and we all went on to celebrate that evening at the Windsor Jazz Festival. The

Who topped the bill, but I was particularly taken with an unknown band called The Move. I could not have imagined that evening that the drummer, Bev Bevan, would one day become a close friend. It was their single, Flowers in the Rain, that a year later became the first record to be played on Radio One.

Those were exciting times for a teenager. I feel really privileged to have grown up during the sixties. The world was changing explosively and pop music seemed to lead the way. I just loved the pirate radio stations out on the North Sea, particularly Radio London. I still have the disc of the final hour after the pirates had been outlawed by the Government. I remember Paul Kay saying, "Big L time is three o'clock and Radio London is now closing down" and out they went to the haunting sounds of Big Lil by Booker T and the MGs. I was on holiday at the time in Abersoch in North Wales, but just managed to pick up the signal by holding the radio to a pipe in someone's kitchen.

Radio London undoubtedly inspired me to think about broadcasting for a career, but I never really thought I would get the chance. It all seemed so remote. The names of the DJs still come easily to mind, including Tony Blackburn, John Peel, Keith Skues, Ed Stewart, Pete Drummond and Tony Windsor. I remember Keith Skues telling us one day to go out and tell our friends that they would be playing the new Beatles double A side Penny Lane and Strawberry Fields every half hour for the rest of the day, even before it had been released.

Ah, the Beatles! The excitement every time they produced a new single or album. You just played it over and over again and, at boarding school, a different Beatle sound seemed to be cascading out of every study along the long dark corridors. I can remember exactly where I was as I first heard All My Loving on the With Beatles LP. The same spot, incidentally, as I was sitting when someone came in and told me President Kennedy had been assassinated.

As we passed the fortieth anniversary of the film A Hard Day's Night in the summer of 2004, it took me back to the first time I saw it. I was on a school camp with our Combined Cadet Force in the Brecon Beacons in south Wales. As a group of us tramped with our fearsome back-packs across those magnificent peaks and valleys, we decided we were desperate to see the film. It was showing not far away in Abergavenny. We descended from the hills, found a main road and hitched a lift on the back of a Coca Cola lorry. We made our way to the cinema, watched the film and loved every minute of it. We eventually joined up with the rest of our contingent to pitch camp for the night, but we had missed a couple of checkpoints during the day, so we were well and truly rumbled. Our punishment has actually had a long term benefit – we had to peel hundreds of potatoes for the rest of the camp and I have been an expert at it ever since.

There was so much terrific music coming out during the sixties, especially from Merseyside, it was an electrifying time to be a teenager. I was also a big Dusty Springfield fan….I even wrote to her, but never received a reply. I told her off years later when I met her at BBC Pebble Mill!

Late in 1966, I headed north to Leeds University to study Classics. I lived first of all with a middle-aged couple in the New Farnley district, not far from the football ground, and a world away from what I had been used to, including Yorkshire pudding on its own and swimming in gravy at the start of Sunday lunch with a nice cup of tea alongside. Violet and Jim Scaife, who looked after me, were terrific. She must have smoked sixty a day and I woke every morning to hear her coughing for England. Jim had a stutter, so conversations were necessarily a lot longer than they might have been. One day, he gave me a lift into university in his Land Rover and the gear stick snapped in his hand. "Niiiiiicholas, bu, bu, bu, bu, bugger's broke!" he said. My first roommate was a lad called Dave. His main interest was beekeeping, so we didn't have too much in common apart from my private sting, but we got on fine. When my mother came to visit once, Violet told her I was a grand lad, but a right little sod!

It took me two bus rides every morning to get to lectures, but that all changed in my second year when I moved to my first flat in Headingley, near the cricket ground and within walking distance of the university. Trevor Butt was my new best friend and we had some sensational times together. We had no power points in the flat, just electric light, no bathroom, just the kitchen sink and use of the loo in the flat downstairs and a measly gas fire which swallowed up our shillings. The mice spent more time there than we did, often leaving their footprints all over the butter. Mind you, in John's flat in the basement, we saw a rat race across the floor as we watched Manchester United win the European Cup, on his flaky old black and white TV.

John was a bit naughty. He collected traffic signs and his room was a tribute to the highways of Great Britain. His bedside light was a Keep Left bollard lit up beautifully from the inside. There were yellow flashing beacons all around the room, but the pièce de résistance following one daring after-dark sortie, was a fully working set of traffic lights – amber included – nicked from some nearby roadworks. He'd had his eye on them for some time. He was an engineer by nature, so he was quite brilliant at adapting the lights to strobe around the room in time with his music. He also covered his wall with tin foil to heighten the effect. Pity really that the police found out and magistrates later relieved him of a few hundred pounds. Four decades on, he's now a balding professor of psychology.

Six of us shared a house the following year, memorable mostly because the drains packed up for nearly a whole term. We had to use facilities across the road where six girls lived. I became very friendly with Janet and I sometimes failed to return from my trips to the loo! I'll never forget my flatmate Derek, who was caught short in a big way at about 3am, and felt he couldn't knock up the girls (so to speak!), so he used a Sunday Express and then took the whole attractive package down the bottom of the garden. A critic even then!

I had some good times at Leeds. I saw the Who, Spencer Davies and the Beach Boys live in their headline years, somehow scraped an honours degree in Classics, despite weeks off with glandular fever, and reached a milestone that most testosterone-packed young boys aspire to before their teens are out. My thanks to Trevor for the loan of his room on that one. I (we) were meant to find it open by accident, a situation slightly undermined when I (we) got inside and found Trevor's note wishing me the best of luck. I was not crazy about the academic life and yearned to get away from hours spent increasingly buried in books in the library. I began to think seriously about journalism and, after a few rejections, I eventually ended up as a graduate trainee on the Doncaster Evening Post.

Chapter Two

REMEMBERING DAVE

The south Yorkshire town of Doncaster may not sound too glamorous from the outside, but it'll always hold a special place in my heart. I enjoyed two and a half of the best years of my life there. I made so many friends in my short time in the town and I hold them dear to this day.

I was lucky when I first went there because I already knew some Doncaster people. John Holt was a close friend at Leeds University, his girl friend (now wife) Lynn Tear used to come and see him at Leeds, and her brother, Dave, became a major part of my life. John and Lynn disappeared off to London soon after I arrived, so Dave and I became an inseparable twosome and enjoyed some wild times on the social scene. Our love life was spectacular – I had a flat, he had a car! We both loved the Beatles and, later, the solo stuff from George Harrison. We played his album, All Things Must Pass, over and over again, particularly My Sweet Lord, which almost became an anthem for us. I will tell you later of a tragedy that followed less than two years down the line and why that song still makes me weep.

My first day in Doncaster was historic, not just for me, but the human race. It was July 21st, 1969, the day Neil Armstrong first walked on the moon. I watched it all in the early hours, so I reported for my first day's work a little bleary-eyed at the converted warehouse that was the Doncaster Evening Post.

"Don't come here with your fancy college ways" was the sort of remark regularly barked across the newsroom floor by some hardened old hack with forty years experience, man and boy, on sixty a day. "Degree in Latin and Greek, what bloody good's that when you're a so-called reporter on t'Post? Get some bloody time in, lad, and then you can call yourself a reporter!"

You were certainly on your own very quickly – I even had a front page story on my first day about the hot weather, helped, I must say, by an impatient chief reporter. I had never touched a typewriter before, so getting to grips with that in itself was quite an ordeal... especially up against a deadline.

I must have covered every golden wedding, council meeting, funeral, bird show, dog show, cat show, cattle show, flower show, any blooming show going that ruined my Saturdays for two and a half years! All for about £12 a week.

Those early days in journalism certainly taught me to think on my feet and be prepared to write a story at a moment's notice. I had so many bollockings from people I thought were absolute bastards, but the lessons were invaluable. We worked some long hours too. Often I would be at a council meeting miles from base till say ten thirty at night, catch the last bus back and then type up as many as ten stories ready to be handed in at the crack of dawn the next day.

I had my first contact with showbiz celebrities in those Doncaster days. I got to know Charlie Williams, the former footballer who became such a hit on the Comedians programme on television, and I interviewed Les Dawson when he was appearing in panto. I must say, fresh out of university, I found it quite exciting meeting people I had seen on the TV. I got to know those two so much better in later years.

I bought my first car in Doncaster. What a disaster that turned out to be! I saw it advertised in my own paper, a Ford Anglia with that weird back window sloping the wrong way, and snapped it up from a prison officer for £75. Dave came with me to pick it up and I drove it back to my place, beaming with pride. Within three hundred yards of the house, we went over a bump and that set the hooter off. It wouldn't stop – so embarrassing as people looked out of their front doors in that quiet suburban road in a pretty decent part of Doncaster. In the end, we decided to switch off the ignition to stop the noise and pushed the car to its new home. Utterly humiliating and not quite the grand arrival I had in mind to impress the neighbours! A technically-minded friend later disconnected the horn, so life continued hooterless but peaceful for a couple of days.

I then took it south to Berkhamsted to show my folks, their garage had it checked and, within minutes of a first cursory look, they told me never to drive it again. Brake pipes were disintegrating merely at a touch, the floor was crumbling and, if I had to take it back to Yorkshire, don't even think of exceeding 30 mph.

Well, I hit 70 all the way, made it safely and got Dave to write a solicitor's letter on headed notepaper, demanding my money back from the guy who had sold it to me. Dave was an articled clerk at the time. No trouble! The prison officer agreed to take it back and he returned the wedge of greenbacks. Cars were one big stress in those days. Every one I ever had seemed to have its problems and I was forever abandoning them when they wouldn't start or spending hours filling in holes on a Sunday!

I continued with my policy of living in dodgy houses and flats! One place was directly opposite the pit gates at Armthorpe, over a bookmaker's. Even with all the windows firmly shut throughout the day, I always found a thick film of coal dust when I returned from work. What that coal dust must have done to the lungs of thousands of miners over the years hardly bears thinking about! That place was a landmark for me, though…I had a phone of my own for the first time. Exciting or what? My mini was broken into one night while I lived there. Unremarkable in one way, I suppose, but what stands out for me was trying to start it the next day. They had stolen my dials, including the oil pressure gauge. So one turn of the engine brought oil gushing forth onto my new, fashionable, pin-striped, wide-lapelled, double-breasted suit, bought only that week for me by my mother for a then gigantic £32! I also shared a house with Mike Massarella, whose father Ronnie managed the Great Britain showjumping team. They're the ice cream family, famous for Mister Softee. Mike had a fabulous black labrador called Trapper. Not so fabulous when he snaffled my meal one night as I turned away to switch on the television.

I took an outside course in journalism while I was at the Doncaster Evening Post, which involved learning shorthand and newspaper law, and eventually passed the proficiency exam which made me a qualified journalist. Life was pretty good and even better when my salary passed the one thousand pounds a year mark!

The euphoria changed quite horrifically on a weekend in early March 1971. I had gone home to Berkhamsted, while Dave was due to go out as usual with his girlfriend on the Saturday night. On the way to her house, he picked up three hitch-hikers looking for a lift to their college near Doncaster. He went out of his way for them, but collided head on with a bus in a country lane and all four in his car were killed outright. The rights and wrongs are hardly relevant today, but my world caved in, as it did for his many friends, and most of all for his family.

I took a call early the next day from my flatmate, Mel Locking, and could hardly take it all in. As I put down the phone, Paul McCartney was singing "It's Just Another Day" on the radio. It certainly wasn't and that haunting song I love and hate in equal measure to this day. I headed north to the Tear's house and found it filled with family and friends of Dave. Absolutely packed. He was much-liked, hugely charismatic, part of a popular local family. His father, Joe, was a well-known businessman, who had been a director of Doncaster Rovers Football Club.

I was asked to write the story for our paper on Monday morning, promptly dissolved and was sent home. I had never known such grief and the funeral service was, inevitably, a terrible ordeal for us all. I was proud to be one of the six young men who carried his coffin. He was only 21. How I felt for his mother, Bessie, his father and two younger sisters, Lynn and Carol. Since then, Bessie has lost Joe and Carol (to breast cancer), but she has remained remarkably resilient. She was always very good to me, as a surrogate mum, when I lived in Doncaster. She made her house like a second home for me and even took me in for a week when I went down with 'flu. I always make contact around March 6th to let her know I am thinking of her.

Mel and I – he was Carol Tear's boyfriend at the time, incidentally – got rid of our flat and went to live with Mel's folks for many months after the tragedy. I won't forget them in a hurry, either.

I also won't forget visiting the site where Dave's ashes were scattered. One sunny Sunday evening, I stood there with a close friend called Iain Ross and, to our amazement, we heard My Sweet Lord drifting across the crematorium from a house nearby. It was quite a moment.

So Doncaster really is a special place for me, but I was ambitious to move on in the newspaper world and eventually landed a job at The Birmingham Post, a prestigious morning paper in the Midlands, which impressed me first of all because the building had lifts. Wow, quality! Mike Massarella organised a superb leaving party for me at Doncaster Airport Club, manning his own disco, and I said farewell to loads of terrific friends at the end of 1971. My favourite pop song at the time was Yellow River by Christie and it was played over and over again that night. If I hear it today, I am instantly transported back to that rousing farewell night. One disgruntled ex-girlfriend, I'm told, gave my car a few hefty kicks during the evening, so I know someone was pleased to see me go! But she and her parents, and many more good folk there, helped me leave with truly wonderful memories of my time in Yorkshire and the start of my working life. Now I was off to the Midlands. The city of Birmingham undoubtedly has a grisly reputation. The centre of a grimy conurbation of heavy industry, next door to the Black Country and all its connotations, a vile view from the traffic jams of the M6 and that much ridiculed accent. Well, I know the accent may take some getting used to, I know you get an appalling impression from the motorway, and Birmingham and the Black Country has indeed been the hub of the country's manufacturing for many years. But, if you have not been before, I suggest you try the place now. It is one of the world's most vibrant and cosmopolitan cities, emerging from a massive renaissance over the last decade. The city centre has been transformed and that process is still going on. It is a very exciting place to be and I am proud to live there, despite my southern roots.

The National Exhibition Centre started the trend of looking towards the Midlands for big business opportunities and it's brought billions of pounds worth of business to the region since the late seventies. The International Convention Centre has grown like a sophisticated sibling within the city centre, now regularly the venue for the CBI conference and acclaimed host for the G8 summit, attended by President Bill Clinton among others in 1998.

The Symphony Hall is renowned across the world, the Royal Ballet is based in the city, major music festivals take place every year

13

in a variety of venues, there is an assortment of theatres, a growing array of bars, restaurants and hotels plus high class sport, including county and Test cricket at Edgbaston, Premiership football and international competition at the National Indoor Arena.

Much of the new development is centred on the city's extensive network of canals, once the lifeline for industry to the rest of the world, now a thriving focal point for business and leisure.

It certainly was not like that when I arrived in January 1972, but I still enjoyed the buzz of a big city after the small town feel of Doncaster. Spaghetti Junction opened in my early days on the newspaper, given the name, as I remember it, by our News Editor, Brian Vertigen, after seeing pictures of it from the air. Its official name is the Gravelly Hill interchange, not quite so catchy.

During those early days, a precocious teenage footballer called Trevor Francis was dominating the football headlines. In fact, he and I were both taking out the same girl for quite a time – she worked on the Post newsdesk. I could not stand the competition after a while, so gracefully withdrew, although we got back together later, became engaged and then drifted apart once more! Trevor, of course, went on to become an England international and the first British player to move for a million pounds. What's more, I was there on that historic occasion – more on that later – and nowadays we see quite a lot of each other because we have so many mutual friends. It was also during those first few months in Birmingham that I was privileged to see the great Pele in action. He was on a tour of the country with his club, Santos of Brazil, and they played Aston Villa at Villa Park.

The match took place during the dark days of the miners' strike, when Edward Heath was Prime Minister. Industry had been forced into a three day week and electricity blackouts had been lasting as long as nine hours. Midweek football matches had to be played in the afternoon, but Aston Villa's chairman, Doug Ellis, managed to hire a generator from Amsterdam. It only had enough power for three of the club's four floodlights and officials had to negotiate with Pele for his agreement for the match to go ahead. The Santos goalkeeper defended the dark end in the first half and was less than delighted to find that Villa had switched the lighting so that he played in the dark end for the second half too! Aston Villa won the match 2-1, with their first goal coming from Pat MacMahon, a classics graduate who had once been a monk! From what I could see, Pele played fairly well and gave the astonishing crowd of over 54,000 value for money. Interesting to reflect that Villa were in the Third Division at the time!

Working on a morning newspaper for the first time meant leisurely mornings before getting to the office for lunchtime and then working through until ten in the evening or sometimes considerably later. By the time we knocked off, the pubs had always closed or were about to, but there were only a handful of places in those days where we could drink late into the night. We mostly went to the Opposite Lock night club off Broad Street and that is where I spent many an hour unwinding after a day's work.

The then owner, Martin Hone, later pioneered motor racing on the streets of Birmingham, after battling for eighteen years to get the idea through Parliament. He staged three spectaculars, as they were called, in the run-up to the racing being given the legal go-ahead and, each time, these attracted crowds of up to 200,000. He also brought along some of the biggest names from the history of motor racing, such as Fangio, Moss and Brabham, to add to the glamour. He envisaged the event as an internationally-recognised festival to energise tourism in the Midlands. To Martin's bitter disappointment, the city council and associates took the event over, but closed it down several years later because they believed it was not economically viable. If Martin had been able to carry it on, I have no doubt it would still be a key part of Birmingham's now-thriving programme of annual festivals. There's still a rather poignant reminder of motor racing in Birmingham, which you can see by the roadside in Bristol Street. For a few weeks each springtime, the crocuses on a grassy bank along the old course spell out the words, Birmingham Super Prix.

I am grateful to a fellow reporter, Rob Kirk, for introducing me during that period to the game of squash, which gave me so much pleasure over the best part of 25 years. Rob and I often used to play tennis in the mornings before going to work at The Birmingham Post. One day, because of the rain, he asked if I had ever played squash. I hadn't, but he soon taught me and I am not sure I have ever played tennis since. I sometimes played three times a week, especially during my days on breakfast television, when it was an ideal way of winding down after the early starts and three hours of live television. It also gave me the chance to play some of the biggest names in the game, when I was filming with them, including Jonah Barrington and Jahangir Khan, both world champions, who hardly broke sweat as I rampaged around the court like a demented rhino. Rob and I, incidentally, later worked together at the BBC and ITV and he is now a power behind the scenes at Sky News.

I was still very much a junior reporter, albeit qualified, and I found some of the work deeply frustrating on The Birmingham Post, so it did not take much to persuade me to consider moving on. I had become friends with Bob Sinkinson, a reporter on the newish local radio station for the West Midlands, BBC Radio Birmingham. We often met on the same stories and he persuaded me that the future lay at Pebble Mill, where there would be much more fun and stimulation than on a newspaper and the salary was astronomical....£2,900 a year! Mind you, I was pretty happy on £1,800 at the Post. In fact, when I left Doncaster and people knew what I would be earning in Birmingham, they were asking how I would be able to handle all that cash!

It took me three assaults on the gruelling BBC interviewing system before I finally made it through the doors of Pebble Mill as a member of staff, joining just a few weeks after Jim Rosenthal, who was to become a close friend and colleague - with a few hiccups along the way - in news and sport, on radio and television. I had enjoyed my time in newspapers, but I was now about to embark on an occupation that has kept me on my toes and happily fulfilled for more than thirty years.

Chapter Three

BOOZING AT THE BARN

In the early seventies, BBC local radio stations were scarce – as were the listeners. They broadcast on VHF or FM, as it is known these days, and that precluded most people from listening because they did not have VHF sets. For want of a better description, those were pioneering, pre-digital days which have led in recent years to an explosion of local stations, BBC and commercial, across the UK.

I remember, in my early days at Pebble Mill, phone-in programmes would drag on interminably before the first call came in. I recall a distinguished actor coming to the studio to answer questions from listeners and, after half an hour, the phones remained stubbornly silent. The presenter and guest were clearly running out of steam. In an act of inspiration, the producer rang round a few people who had made calls in recent weeks, furnished them with questions and slapped them on air! It was all very heavy going, with a feeling that we were sometimes talking in a vacuum, but still nerve-wracking to go on air for the first time. The bosses were listening, if no-one else!

My first live broadcast was a news bulletin in the early morning during the Les Ross show. He was the most popular and best-known figure on the station. He has since gone on to become an institution in the Midlands, presenting the breakfast show for the commercial station, BRMB, for a quarter of a century, and, more recently, moving to Saga FM. I can still remember the feeling of abject fear as he introduced me…heart thumping away, hands dripping with sweat. I have no doubt that I had a monotonous voice with little light or shade as I ensured firstly that I got the words right without stumbling. My news editor, Martin Henfield, told me at one stage to try to sound more interested!

I was finding it quite tough adjusting to my new world, which included hi-tech activities (for me!) such as using a tape recorder, and the love life was a bit rocky at the time. I started to feel a little nervous about things, I developed rashes and the doctor put me on Valium. I covered a football match at Aston Villa and a colleague complained that I sounded as if I was half asleep. I dumped the tranquillizers.

Talking about tape recorders, I smile when I recall my first interview. It was with the leader of Birmingham City Council, Clive Wilkinson, and I was so nervous that I grunted at the end of each of Clive's answers, as if adding my own punctuation. I had not yet learned the art of editing audio tape with a razor blade, so, as time was pressing, a colleague had to be commandeered to hack out the offending interruptions. The guy, who rescued the interview, was our union leader at the time, who later went into party politics and now resides on the top table of the Labour Party, Denis MacShane.

Two particular news stories stand out in the memory....extremely sad ones, too. Two young cousins, both boys, whose families shared a house, had disappeared one evening in a canal area near the centre of Birmingham. I was sent down the following morning to find out whether the police had tracked them down. I arrived as they were trawling the canal in the area where they had last been seen and, tragically, a body was soon pulled out of the water. I rang the news editor, who told me to record a report for the 11 o'clock news which was due in about fifteen minutes time. After I had finished that, he told me to visit the home of the families nearby, which I did with some trepidation. The father of one of the boys opened the door and asked if I knew anything. What could I say? I took the easy option and said I knew nothing at this stage, but asked if I could come in for a chat. I entered the huge living room, filled with distressed and anxious relatives. I bluffed my way through, but I was acutely aware that our radio station was blaring out from the mantlepiece. As the news jingle played at eleven and the newsreader said "We've just heard...", I walked over and turned it off. I couldn't bear the thought of my telling them the awful news over the radio, while I was actually there with them in the room. I somehow managed to get an interview from one of the parents about the stress of not knowing what had happened and went. Two police officers were at the door, as I left, presumably to break the terrible news. It was revealed later that the other little lad had drowned as well. The whole dreadful episode left a deep impression upon me and I shall never forget the surreal experience of being in the room with the families and being about to hear myself tell them over the radio the news they were dreading. Those little boys would have been in their forties by now.

The kidnapping of 17-year-old Shropshire heiress Lesley Whittle captured headlines around the world. She disappeared overnight in mid-January 1975 from the family home in Highley, near Bridgnorth. She had been taken from her bed, while her mother slept. Lesley had been left £82,000 by her father who had founded the Whittle coach company and that was assumed to be the reason she had been taken. A ransom note on Dymo tape was left behind in the house, demanding £50,000. In the early stages, police thought the whole episode might have been a hoax, but tragically that was not the case. I was the first radio reporter to get to the house that morning and filed a report for Radio Four as well our own station, Radio Birmingham. I met Lesley's brother, Ronald, and spoke to him at their front door, but he was not prepared to give an interview.

Ronald Whittle followed instructions to take money to a phone box, but no-one ever came and the search became more frantic with every passing day. There was some contact with the kidnapper and police constantly monitored Ronald's movements, but a rendezvous never took place. At the same time, detectives were tackling a spate of post office raids and murders and I remember wondering if they could all be the work of the same person. It seemed unlikely until a press release came over the wires at our newsroom to announce a joint press conference the next day involving police from both investigations. They were indeed now both looking for the same man. He became known as the Black Panther because of his trademark balaclava, the most wanted man in Britain. The most pressing need at this stage was to find Lesley, but it was looking increasingly bleak.

I was at home with my folks for a few days when news came out that Lesley had been found dead. She was hanging from a wire at the bottom of a drainage shaft in Bathpool Park, Kidsgrove in Staffordshire. It seemed she had been there from day one, in complete darkness, with a sleeping bag and some food, but secured by that awful wire. She died either because she had fallen or been pushed over the edge by her kidnapper.

As with many colleagues, I had become quite emotionally involved with the story of this innocent college student who must have suffered such misery and abject fear. How anyone can perpetrate such a vile crime defies understanding. I realise you can say that about a multitude of appalling incidents through the history of time – it just happens that the murder of Lesley Whittle particularly touched me because I had been drawn in from the start and because it was the first time as a reporter I had become close to a murder story. I still shudder when I see signs for Kidsgrove off the M6 motorway.

In December that year, two police officers in Mansfield in Nottinghamshire saw a man acting suspiciously. They approached him and he pulled a gun on them. After some difficulty and help from customers at a fish and chip shop, he was arrested. Thanks to alert policing, the Black Panther had been caught. He turned out to be Donald Neilson from Yorkshire and the evidence from his home was overwhelming. In July, 1976, he was sent down with five life sentences for the murder of Lesley, killing three post office workers, burglary and abduction.

One quirky postscript to the affair. On that night of great excitement at Mansfield Police Station when Neilson was arrested, a young constable was on duty who later changed careers and became Coventry City's mountain of a goalkeeper, and a mate, Steve Ogrizovic!

Our sports programmes were far and away the most popular on the station. The sports producer when I arrived, Roger Moody, soon left for the BBC's Match of the Day and Jim Rosenthal took over, with me as his unofficial second-in-command. I covered countless matches and did a fair amount of presenting on Saturdays in the studio, fantastic practice for copious amounts of live television in the future. I thought Jim was a master, even then, though he was still relatively inexperienced. Superb voice, terrific interviewing technique and excellent presenting skills, attributes that have served him so well ever since.

Jim and I became close, through work, to a number of footballers and cricketers and our Thursday nights out were legendary. The cast list often included Jim Cumbes, John Gidman,

Chico Hamilton and Ian Ross of Aston Villa, Bob Willis and David Brown of Warwickshire plus various other reprobates from our social circle. Jim Cumbes, incidentally, was also a professional cricketer, who played for Lancashire, Surrey, Worcestershire and Warwickshire in his career. He was one of the last to be able to combine football and cricket at top level. We used to frequent a small private hotel, the Binton Barn in Edgbaston, which locked its doors late on and we were privileged to be able to stay on until well after midnight. They had a right old character there called Len Newberry on piano, churning out his enormous repertoire of lewd ditties on request. How the Villa lads had the strength and inclination for a rigorous training session on Friday mornings I will never know. I remember Jim lying unconscious on my bathroom floor at 3am, a mere six hours before reporting for duty at Villa's windswept and unappetising training ground, Bodymoor Heath.

One particular regular at the Binton was old Jinx Bagley. He suffered a stroke at the early age of 37 and was given six months to live. He lived as if he had six months to go for another 47 years! He had only one eye that worked after allegedly being kicked by a horse. He wore glasses and his dodgy eye had an opaque lens, like a toilet window. His left arm was useless after the stroke, but it twitched around relentlessly and gave the girls quite a surprise when he got close and personal up at the bar. He had a special monologue which he recited around midnight every Thursday by public demand. Most of it is unrepeatable here, but I can just about get away with the first verse:

> The portions of a woman that appeal to a man's depravity,
> Are fashioned with considerable care.
>
> And what to you and me appears a simple cavity,
> Is really a quite elaborate affair.

The rest was very naughty, graphic and hilarious. He always got a standing ovation from those who were still equipped to stand. Jinx died when he was 84.

Cumbesie was a particular friend. His charismatic personality made him an obvious choice to front his own show on Radio Birmingham and this he did on a Sunday morning, a mix of music, requests and interviews with listeners. We had some great nights out both in Birmingham and London, but he himself was quite a party-giver in his own right, especially with his amazing fancy dress events. I went once as a chicken which took some pluck. He loved Bonfire Night. Hundreds of pounds worth of fireworks lit the night sky behind his small maisonette in Edgbaston, but one ended disastrously when a rocket shot across the garden at head level and hit Villa full-back John Gidman in the eye. It was a gruesome incident and it seemed likely John would lose his sight in that eye, but somehow it was restored almost to full working order. He was out for half the season, though, and missed Villa's victory in the 1975 League Cup Final against Norwich City.

Jim Cumbes is now Chief Executive at Lancashire Cricket Club, but he holds a record that straddles football and cricket. He is the only sportsman to have won a cricket county championship (with Worcestershire) and a league cup final (Aston Villa) in adjoining seasons - within a six month period, in fact. Another goalkeeper, Jim Standen, achieved something similar a decade previously, when he won the FA Cup with West Ham and then the championship with Worcestershire. Unthinkable now, isn't it?

It was through my sporting circle that I first met the woman who was to become my wife. Jill Lavery, a ward sister at the Queen Elizabeth Hospital in Birmingham, was the girlfriend of Warwickshire and England fast bowler Bob Willis, when I first met her at the cricket club's supporters' bar. Bob was away touring in the West Indies and I was committed at the time, so it was just a casual first meeting amongst a group of friends. I did not think much more of it and Jill barely remembers it! We bumped into each other on and off after that, but it was not until three years later in 1976, long after she and Bob had parted, that I first asked her out. I had just come to the end of an extremely happy couple of years with Mandy, but we had fallen out and gone our separate ways. I actually asked Jill out for the first time at the Binton Barn and she accompanied me to one of Jim's famous fancy dress parties two days later. We married in Edgbaston in the summer of 1977. The first of our four children, Andy, arrived in 1979, followed by Tim, two years later, then a break for breakfast television before we reopened the production line with Chris in 1986 and Jenny in 1988.

Predictably, they have all inherited my passion for sport, but the talent has definitely come from their mother. They have all had their successes on the field, whether in football, cricket, hockey or netball and that ability has undoubtedly derived from Jill, a fine runner as a youngster, who was stopped quite literally in her tracks by a blood-curdling injury. She tripped on a piece of stone during a sprint in a county event, fell head over heels and her spikes ripped a huge gash in her thigh. Bearing in mind where we first met, it's interesting that our first son, Andy, now works behind the scenes at Warwickshire County Cricket Club and both he and Tim have represented the county at various levels.

Sport became a major part of my work with Radio Birmingham and, when Jim Rosenthal left for network radio in London, I took over as the station's sports producer. It was quite a demanding job with a lot of output; bulletins at each end of every day, a half hour programme on Friday night and about five hours live on Saturday. I could hire in help, of course, at the magnificent figure of £6 a day, but, basically, it was all down to me. I thrived on it, though it could be quite exhausting getting round all the grounds for interviews during the week, reporting live on midweek matches and fronting many of the programmes as well.

For much of the time, five of our six football clubs were in the top division. Aston Villa, Birmingham City, Coventry City, West Bromwich Albion and Wolves. I was dealing with managers such as Ron Saunders, Freddie Goodwin, Jim Smith, Alf Ramsey, Gordon Milne, Johnny Giles, Ron Atkinson, Ronnie Allen, Sammy Chung and Bill McGarry, to name but a few. In rugby, Coventry and Moseley were two of the very best clubs, while the county cricket sides of Warwickshire and Worcestershire fielded some magical names including Dennis Amiss, John Jameson and Rohan Kanhai at Edgbaston, with Glenn Turner, Imran Khan and Basil d'Oliveira at

New Road, Worcester. Summer afternoons commentating at those grounds were always an utter joy.

European football took me abroad with Aston Villa and West Bromwich Albion and some great trips we had too. I shall always be haunted, though, by Villa's trip to Poland to meet Gornik Zabrze in November 1977. We arrived on my birthday, and, as we headed in the dark for our hotel, our coach driver was stopped by a police officer for speeding. He was sent happily on his way, though, by a deluge of Villa souvenirs! It was All Saints Day when Polish families traditionally visited their local cemeteries and lit candles by the graves. It was an awesome sight through the towns and villages, as we passed scores of cemeteries during our two hour journey from the airport to Katowice, with up to thirty flames burning at each grave.

It was fairly cold, particularly on the evening of the game. I had never had vodka before in my life, but I was mighty grateful for a bottle of the fearsome local stuff by my side as my friend, Graham Clarke, Editor of the Villa Times, and I commentated at a table actually on the grass. We drank it neat and it sure helped keep out the cold night air sweeping in from the Ukraine to the east. Andy Gray, now renowned for his expert views on Sky Sports, scored the goal that took Villa through to the next round. We were fogged in that night, so we had to prolong our stay in Krakow in the hope we could take off for home the next morning. In the reception area of the Holiday Inn, in front of players and a few well-heeled supporters, I asked manager Ron Saunders for permission to interview Andy. He said "No. You always want to interview the glamour boys. You can talk to Frank Carrodus." Well, Frank was a great bloke and a tireless worker in midfield, but he was not the story. Saunders and I had a stand-up argument in the hotel foyer before I walked off, wondering why he was always such a pain. He is undoubtedly the most difficult man I have ever had to deal with. Easy, I suppose, to intimidate a young reporter, trying to do his job. It was not the first time. Luckily, Andy had heard it all, pulled me to one side and told me to meet up in his room to do the interview there, which we did.

What haunts me to this day, though, is a visit many of us made during that trip to the Auschwitz concentration camp, which was not far away. The camp had been left exactly as it was found by the Russian army in 1945. I came out of that dank, dark and dismal hell-hole feeling I would never complain about anything again. Anyone who has made the tour will know how graphic and vivid are the accounts of the dreadful suffering meted out by that sickening Nazi regime. No-one will ever be certain exactly how many died there, but the most conservative estimate these days is just over one million, with some believing the figure is as high as an almost incomprehensible four million. I have interviewed survivors since then and I am always amazed at their mental strength and resilience. Our party of Villa club officials, led by Doug Ellis, journalists and supporters left in horrified silence.

Villa's European excursions that season ended in Barcelona. The first leg in early March saw a two-all draw at Villa Park, when Villa scored two in the last four minutes after a masterclass earlier in the game from Johann Cruyff. They lost 2-1 at the Nou Camp in the return leg in front of 80,000. The players took to the field past that famous chapel in the tunnel....full-back John Gidman saw it again much sooner than he expected. After a litany of fouls against him, he lashed out in retaliation only 21 minutes into the game and was sent off. The dream was over for the time being, but three years later Villa club landed the big one, the European Cup.

I cannot leave the subject of Aston Villa and my radio days without saying more about Andy Gray. He signed from Dundee United for £110,000 in October 1975 and became an absolute sensation for the club. He joined what was fast emerging into a superb side in the seventies, highlighted for me by a truly memorable match they played against Liverpool in December 1976. Liverpool were the cream of Europe at the time and current English champions, who had beaten Villa 3-0 at Anfield only a few weeks earlier. A crowd of nearly 43,000 on that Wednesday evening at Villa Park saw an utterly mesmerising performance. They were five-one up at half time, with two goals each from Gray and John Deehan, plus one from Brian Little....and that against a team that included Kevin Keegan and Emlyn Hughes. It was a privilege to be reporting on it for radio...in fact, it was just a privilege to be there at all.

I first met two great comedians through sport, Eric Morecambe and Jasper Carrott. Both were guests on my Saturday programme. Eric was working at Pebble Mill on a television show, but he took time out, when I invited him up to our radio studio, and chatted away about his love of football for about an hour. I think he is just about the best of all time, but the added ingredient for me is the fact that he supported my team, Luton Town. I was to interview him again some years later on breakfast television. Obviously, we didn't know it then, but that second meeting at TVam took place in the final weeks of his wonderful life. As for Jasper, he joined me as a special guest for about three hours just as his career was about to take off in a big way. He was making a serious name for himself in the Midlands and it was spreading across the nation, he had an album out and his Funky Moped/Magic Roundabout single was climbing the charts. He has since become a very good friend.

I always imagined I would end up presenting sport on national radio, but a one-off opportunity sent me away on a tangent I had not foreseen. I was supplying reports and interviews on a regular basis to my colleagues in London, the likes of Des Lynam, Christopher Martin-Jenkins and Jim Rosenthal, of course, and had not even contemplated a move into television when I was offered the chance to front a single half-hour programme for BBC Midlands TV to mark the dawn of a new football season. This was in August 1977 and I was only invited because the man they had in mind, Tony Francis, then a freelance in the television newsroom, was going to be away on holiday. I jumped at the chance, but never for a moment saw it as the start of a new direction in my life. I presented the show with a friend called Peter Windows, a fellow classicist, by chance, who worked as a continuity announcer and had a great interest in sport. He is now a lecturer in journalism after a spell producing the Archers. The programme went well and I virtually forgot about it. Life continued as normal in radio, until I bumped into footballing legend Billy Wright some time later at a match. Billy, former captain of Wolves and England, was then head of sport at ATV, the Midlands commercial channel, and he was generous in his praise for my efforts a few weeks earlier. He and his colleague, Trevor East, followed it up a few months afterwards with an offer to join them as a reporter/presenter at ATV. I actually had confirmation of that when I was in Izmir in Turkey for a West Bromwich Albion UEFA Cup match. I was sitting having coffee in a beach café with Bob Mills, my opposite number from Birmingham's commercial radio station BRMB, when I called my wife, Jill, who told me a letter had arrived from Billy. I was slightly nervous at leaving a secure staff post with the BBC for a short contract with the other side, in a medium I knew very little about. Bob was extremely encouraging, saying television would suit me down to the ground. He was a real mate and I knew I could trust him. Why? Because when I had the runs at a football ground in Istanbul some years earlier and there was no paper in the stadium toilets, he ripped up half his notebook for me! True friendship!

So it was then that I left BBC local radio in November 1978 to make the short trip down the road to ATV and an intriguing new phase of my life. My last live interview on my Saturday afternoon sports programme was with goalkeeper Jim Cumbes, after Worcester City's battling second round FA Cup tie. They had drawn away to Newport, so they were in the hat for a possible glamour draw in the Third Round. My first interview for television came forty eight hours later, on the Monday, following that draw for the next round. If they could win their replay, Worcester would meet mighty West Ham United. And who did I talk to? Obvious, isn't it? Jim Cumbes, of course!

Chapter Four

THE JOY OF THE CUP

Walking into the offices of ATV for the first time was not as daunting as it might have been because I bumped into so many familiar faces. There was Billy Wright, for a start, one of the greatest international footballers of all time. One hundred and five caps for England, most of them as captain, immense success as skipper of Wolverhampton Wanderers when they were one of the very top clubs in the country; an icon, in fact, whose autograph I was thrilled to secure as a ten year old when he played a charity match for a Showbiz XI in my home town of Berkhamsted. Now, he was head of ATV Sport and I was about to get his signature every week.... on my expenses form!

Then there was Gary Newbon, the sports presenter, who was already well known in the Midlands. It was not long before he told me he felt I did not have much future as a presenter or interviewer – it would be better to concentrate on commentating. As for Gary himself, let's just say you would never see the words Newbon and shrinking violet in the same sentence.

Our sports editor was Trevor East, an extremely talented producer and dynamic ideas man, who now handles Rupert Murdoch's cheque book for sport. He is Deputy Managing Director, Commercial and Acquisitions at Sky Sports, buying up sporting events around the world. He was also, at the time, a familiar face on television as one of the manic presenters of the Saturday morning children's programme, Tiswas.

And, talking about Tiswas, one of the reporters at ATV was none other than its main presenter, Chris Tarrant. Larger than life, he careered through the newsroom like a whirlwind. You always knew when he was around. His speciality on the ATV Today news programme was the off-the-wall character, the off-beat story that could lighten the mood at the end of a gruelling day's news. He described himself as "rent-a-c**t".

He tells a great story about those days. He used to receive a regular stream of fan mail from adoring females, including one who said she would like to stick her hand in his trousers. He showed the letter to our Editor Mike Warman, who hatched a plan. When Chris was out filming, Mike sneaked into his dressing room, found Chris's only suit and pilfered the trousers. He parcelled them up and sent them off to the unsuspecting admirer with a note that said, "Now you can put your hand in his trousers as often as you like!"

Working alongside Mike Warman was managing editor Ted Trimmer, a typical old school journalist and a pioneer of regional independent television. A lovely, jovial man who always wore a bow tie, he delighted in telling us anecdotes about his days in Fleet Street and his Hollywood connections. His older sister was the Oscar nominated actress, Deborah Kerr, who starred in the film 'The King And I'. Tragically, Ted died at the age of 78 in the summer of 2004 after he had been punched in the face during an apparent road rage attack.

Our angling expert, Terry Thomas, was a great friend of Chris and a great friend of pub landlords everywhere. He was a sort of middle-aged country gent, who wore tweeds, and sported a moustache in the centre of an often very red face. He was a terrific character and a superbly relaxed broadcaster, with an elegant turn of phrase. His live, ad-lib voice-overs to accompany some beautiful film around the rivers of the Midlands were a joy to listen to. But one day, I was not sure we would get to hear him. I was about to present a football item in the studio, when I sensed a gentle moaning beside me. The whine became louder into a good old snore and I realised that Terry had nodded off, although he was due on just after me. As I was delivering my piece, I was aware of the floor manager's frantic efforts to revive him, which he did, and Terry presented seconds later as immaculately as ever!

There was an almost tangible buzz about ATV in Birmingham because so much seemed to be going on. Any friends who came to visit me always wanted to look round the Crossroads set and the soap actors and actresses themselves were always around for a chat. I would regularly find myself sitting next to the likes of Noele Gordon, Jane Rossington or Paul Henry in make-up. Another Crossroads performer was Sue Hanson and, through her, I came to know her husband Carl Wayne, well known as a singer with the Move. He was always good company and I remember much later how thrilled he was to have joined the Hollies. I was shattered when he died of cancer within a few days of Ted Trimmer.

Derek Hobson, later to find fame fronting New Faces, was the main presenter of ATV Today, with his on-air manner of gentle Irish calm and charm. Other new colleagues included my old schoolfriend, Bob Warman, a reporter/presenter, and Peter Plant, who later became my agent.

Derek Hobson introduced me for my first-ever live slot on commercial television on my first day there on a November Monday in 1978. Gary was off having a small operation on his eyes, so it fell to me to deliver a six minute round-up of the day's events. Besides interviewing Jim Cumbes, I had also recorded earlier in the day a film piece with swimming gold medallist, David Wilkie, about Olympic sponsorship. I saw David many times after that, most memorably when we competed against each other over the assault course in a special Olympic celebrity edition of the Krypton Factor! But that is jumping ten years.

My second day at ATV stands out for me because of a story that, today, would not raise an eyebrow. For the first time, England had picked a black footballer for international duty – full-back Viv Anderson of Nottingham Forest. I discussed his merits on the programme over action pictures with Billy Wright and, a day later, Viv, known as the Spider because of his long, rangy legs, made his debut against Czechoslovakia. It seems truly remarkable now, doesn't it, that a black player hit the headlines because he had been picked for England?

In regional terms, ATV covered a wide area. On the outer circle, I made frequent trips to Mansfield, Lincoln, Stoke, Shrewsbury, Hereford, Swindon and Oxford, with Nottingham, Leicester, Derby, Coventry, Wolverhampton and, of course, Birmingham much nearer to base. In those days, you needed to get back in good time from an assignment, because your film needed to be processed in another part of Birmingham and that could take an hour before a dispatch rider delivered it to the studio. Then the editing could start. One of those dispatch riders was Mike Inman, who knew so much about motor bikes that he used to come with me when I covered speedway meetings and give me expert advice. He also used to babysit for us. He is now one of ITV Sport's top producers.

In little over two months from the time that I started at ATV, Birmingham City's star striker Trevor Francis moved to Nottingham Forest. It was the country's first million pound transfer and I was right there at the City Ground, Nottingham, as the historic deal took place. I was due to give an as-live report on proceedings and then interview the great Brian Clough, the Forest manager. As-live means the whole operation is treated as live, even though it takes place a few minutes before transmission. There is no time to edit, although it does go down on videotape.

I knew Trevor and his wife, Helen, well, but it was my first meeting with Clough. Inevitably, I was a little anxious. Momentous occasion as it was, Clough was still dressed in his squash gear after playing earlier in the afternoon. "Are you OK, young man?" he asked in his familiar, idiosyncratic twang. "Well, I'm a bit nervous," I replied. "Don't worry, I'll look after you," he said. At which point, he rammed his squash racket straight into my crutch! And that is why, on this record-breaking occasion for English football, the reporter with the television exclusive, probably had a hint of a tear running down his cheeks!

I interviewed Brian Clough many times over the ensuing years, both for ATV and Central Sport and for ITV Sport nationally. Never a bore, always a challenge. He could be charm itself, call you into his office, share half a bottle of scotch and then bawl you out for no apparent reason in front of a load of startled onlookers the very next day. I remember one time he had spent about an hour having a heart-to-heart with me in his office and, the very next afternoon, just before a match kicked off, he told me to "f**k off" out of the ground. The stewards had no option but to ease me on my way! Bless him! Another time, he was so tired and emotional when we went to interview him for ITV's On the Ball, we had to give the whole thing a miss. Inevitably, he has mellowed in recent times and, when I met up with him again not so long ago at a funeral, he was utterly enchanting company. He certainly brightened the landscape of English football for many decades and he is rightly regarded as a hero in the north east, where he played with such distinction, and in Nottingham and Derby, where he landed remarkable success as a manager. I also enjoyed some convivial moments and terrific interviews with Brian Clough's managerial partner, Peter Taylor. It is tragic that they fell out so badly and broke off contact after all their phenomenal triumphs together, but strangely comforting that Clough slipped in quietly at the back of the church for Peter's funeral. Peter's daughter, Wendy, is an old friend and her husband, John Dickinson, has been a mate and work-colleague over many years.

Before I had been with ATV for a year, the whole of ITV went on strike over plans to introduce new technology. The National Union of Journalists had no direct part in it, but we were laid off. On the day the stoppage came to an end after three months, ITV Sport nationally decided to show highlights of a Forest European Cup match against the Romanian side, Arges Pitesti. ATV's regular commentator, Hugh Johns, could not make the game in time from his home in South Wales, so I was pitched in with just hours to go before kick-off. I had no time for serious research about the opposition, but the Romanian ambassador happened to be at the City ground for the match and he briefed me beautifully. I hope I did the occasion justice, but it was a bit of a scramble for one so new to television.

I never fancied myself as a commentator, although I had plenty of opportunities to have a go. In those days, it was far more difficult for the man with the microphone because there were rarely slow motion replays available during the match itself. These were put into the edited version afterwards. In other words, to describe a crucial moment that had just happened for a slow motion replay later, the commentator had to recall from memory the detail of the move leading up to the incident. Nowadays, of course, the commentator and expert can see it again almost immediately.

I spent many days editing football through Saturday night into Sunday morning for ATV's Star Soccer, which was broadcast on the

Sunday afternoon. There would be highlights of our own chosen game and bites from a couple of other matches filmed in other regions. We would record these in the course of the evening during a mass play-out. One of the more time-consuming aspects of the job was having to play sequences down the line to a company in London who had an action replay machine. They would record what we sent and then play them back up the line in the form we wanted! We would always be praying that the commentary from Hugh Johns matched the finished product and it usually did. He was a highly professional operator and really good guy to work with, always supportive.

Despite my reservations, I was asked to commentate on Group 3 in the 1982 World Cup in Spain, although my main task was to file reports. I spent as much time as I could visiting training camps in the area around Alicante to familiarise myself with the players from Argentina, Belgium, El Salvador and Hungary. Mind you, nothing could have prepared me for the first match I covered. Hungary stuffed El Salvador 10-1 at Elche! That is a lot of goals to get right, when none of the players were exactly household names to a part-time English commentator! The most memorable game for me in the group was Argentina against Hungary, which the South Americans won 4-1. The Argentina star that night was a young man I had never seen in the flesh before, one Diego Maradona. He was sensational, dominating the play and scoring two of the goals. I recall leaving the stadium with sports journalist Ian Woolridge and we both agreed we had witnessed the best footballer in the world at that time. Ossie Ardiles scored a goal too that evening. Later, I interviewed him at their training camp. All went well until I changed the subject to the mood of the players, in the light of the Falklands War which had just ended in defeat for Argentina. He backed away and virtually clammed up. The armed guards closed in and looked particularly menacing. The crew and I diplomatically terminated our chat!

I made a serious blunder when I commentated on an Aston Villa-Coventry City evening match early in my television career. It was a bitterly cold night and I treated myself to a couple of lagers an hour or so before kick-off. Then it was up the ladder to Villa Park's wonky old gantry, where I would be stationed with the crew for at least the next three hours. Football ground gantries in those days were fairly basic structures, made largely of planks and scaffolding. You needed to be up there in good time, so the ladder could be pulled up to enable the crowd to reach their seats unhindered. After only twenty minutes of the match, I realised I had a little problem. That lager was starting to make its presence felt in the bladder region. How would I make it to the end of the game without going to the loo? By the second half, I was in real discomfort...so much so I was forced to stand up to relieve the pressure! By the end of the match, I was utterly desperate but still no relief because the crowd stuck around to hear the rest of the night's results. For health and safety reasons (but not mine!), the ladder had to stay firmly up with us in the gantry. Luckily, I had an understanding bunch of colleagues and they scoured the rubbish-strewn gantry on my behalf. Thus it was I fell to my knees and, high above thousands of unknowing fans, managed to fill thirteen polystyrene cups and so restore my sanity. Not so sure about the dignity! Every time I hear "ladder" I also think of "bladder"!

I was lucky enough to be sent as ITV Sport's reporter to the European Championships in Italy in 1980, when England goalkeeper Ray Clemence had bladder problems of a different sort. I was due to interview him after the Spain match in Naples, but he had also been chosen for a random drugs test. As is often the case after hectic athletic activity, especially in a hot country, he was as dry as a Bedouin's sandal. We had to wait ages before he emerged alone from the dressing room long after his team-mates had headed off to their hotel. Ever the gent, he gave me an interview on England's 2-1 victory. Oh, and the test was all clear!

Getting to the players you wanted on match days was not always easy. Producer Trevor East and I hoped to interview Peter Shilton after the game against Italy in Turin, but we had not been able to make contact with him in advance. Somehow we blagged our way past security a couple of hours before kick-off and sneaked into the England dressing room. We found the team kit laid out on the benches and stuffed a note inside Shilton's jersey. Bang on cue, he came out to meet us after the match, which England lost 1-0. It was at Turin that the England fans rioted behind one of the goals and the local police sprayed them with tear gas. The wind swept it towards the media in the main stand, an extremely uncomfortable experience for us all.

In 1981, the awarding of the ITV franchises deemed that ATV should split into two and give the East Midlands its own committed team and headquarters. So Central East and Central West were born and I was asked to move to Nottingham to be the main male presenter there for news and sport, alongside a young woman colleague called Anne Diamond. I did not know Anne too well at that stage, but she had already made her mark as one to watch, both as a reporter and presenter.

We were described by Central as two of the company's brightest young stars and, from that moment on, we were pitched together in a partnership that lasted on and off, through highs and lows, for about fifteen years. We spent a huge amount of time together, publicising our new show and rehearsing in the studio. We used temporary studios at Giltbrook, outside Nottingham, but a new, state-of-the-art building was planned for Lenton Lane near the city centre. When it finally opened long after Anne and I had moved on, it proved to be the last word in broadcasting facilities. It is ironic to reflect that only twenty years later it was deemed obsolete and Central said they were leaving.

For Anne and me, the move to Nottingham was our big break. It enabled us to come out of the shadows of more established presenters in Birmingham and we had a terrific time building up to our launch in January 1981. Unfortunately, ATV's transformation into Central meant closing the company's prestigious studios at Elstree, where many of ATV's best known programmes had been made, such as the Muppets and Celebrity Squares. It brought staff into conflict with management over the terms and conditions of the move north and the dispute came to a head at the worst possible moment. On the day scheduled for our first programme, the technicians pulled the plug, so we broadcast our show only to gathered dignitaries and colleagues within a radius of twenty yards! It was all very dismal and a dreadful anti-climax.

We continued doing dummy programmes for about six weeks and had some great times. As far as Anne and I were concerned, the situation strengthened our growing friendship and we learned a lot about presenting in partnership. Ultimately, it made us yearn for our own show together one day, even if it was not going to be in Nottingham. Overall, though, the picture was rather demoralising and management made it clear they could see no immediate settlement of the dispute by decreeing that Anne and I should return to Birmingham and join forces with the team there. Central West was up and running successfully, with Wendy Nelson and Bob Warman as main presenters. We were to split duties with them on a show that was now covering East and West Midlands, not what the Independent Broadcasting Authority had in mind at all. For my part, there was also the sporting side of the equation as well. I was now unofficially number three sports presenter in Birmingham behind Gary Newbon and Bob Hall and, more than once, there was no room for me in the half hour sports programme that went out every Friday evening. Anne and I found ourselves underused and it was all very frustrating. Bob Warman was not too crazy about the situation either and complained that Anne and Nick were on too often for his liking. In fact, on one occasion, to keep the peace, Anne and I were taken out of rehearsals late afternoon and sent home. We both decided we had to move on, as there was no immediate prospect of Central East taking to the airwaves. Eventually, Anne joined BBC Nationwide in London and I approached a former work colleague, Paul Vaughan, who had become an agent. I asked him to look out for a job that could take me away from the frustration and uncertainty of Central. Within a couple of weeks, I was heading south for the dawn of breakfast television.

I had not given breakfast television much thought in the months before it was due to go on air. I thought it would be irrelevant because I could not see how people would be bothered with watching a television programme at that time of day. I never for a minute thought I would become involved, but my opinion changed completely by chance. As I have said, I felt underemployed at Central, so I suggested I flew out to Australia to put together a special feature on the England cricketers on their Ashes tour. To my delight, I got the go-ahead, but I would not be there long. I had about two and a half days in Adelaide, sandwiched between the flights and two bus journeys between Birmingham and Heathrow. The England squad was full of Midland players I knew fairly well and I was made to feel very welcome, particularly by the captain and old friend, Bob Willis. I raced around with the Australian crew, filming the cricketers off duty with wives and girlfriends, while those who were alone recorded Christmas messages for their families back home. I watched some of the Adelaide Test in sweltering heat and returned with a peeling nose to find Birmingham in a blizzard. But, during my few days down under, I saw breakfast television for the first time and it really caught my imagination. I felt it was the sort of programme that would suit me down to the ground, so it seemed an astonishing coincidence when I received a call from Paul Vaughan, saying TVam were due on air in four weeks time and needed a sports presenter. Was I interested? You bet I was.

While Anne Diamond became an enduring friend through breakfast television and beyond, someone else came into my life at ATV who was due to share a fair number of experiences with me in the ensuing years. One Jimmy Greaves. He had visited Birmingham to publicise his book about his battle against alcoholism and I was only too pleased to interview him. I had watched him from the terraces in his glory years with Chelsea and Tottenham Hotspur, now I was meeting a childhood hero in the flesh. He gave me his phone number and when, later, ITV got the contract to broadcast football highlights on Saturday evenings, Billy Wright and company considered having Jimmy as an expert analyst. I duly supplied his telephone number and Trevor East called him up, but Jimmy hesitated a bit because of his commitments to the Sun newspaper. Finally, to the satisfaction of all involved, a deal was done and Jimmy set out on a whole new career for himself in television. We worked closely together at ATV/Central and then later, at national level, with TVam and ITV Sport.

When Jim started working for ATV, I used to spend a lot of time chatting to him about his remarkable goalscoring career and his ensuing battle with the bottle. Despite my misgivings, we often went to the bar in the run-up to the Saturday evening show and he always said he was quite happy to see me sink a pint, while he made do with a coke or lemonade! It could not have been easy for him, though, and I have tremendous regard for the willpower he has shown for well over twenty five years since he downed his last alcoholic drink. He was also good enough to help others. A close friend of mine was going through a dreadful time with drink in the early eighties and asked me if he could meet Jim. Jim agreed immediately and my friend duly came to the studios. They spent at least an hour together in Jim's dressing room and the advice he gave helped enormously. That friend has been mostly dry since then and he is eternally grateful for the time Jim gave him during his darkest days.

When I announced I was leaving Central for TVam, my sanity was universally questioned. Billy Wright and Trevor East both said I was crazy and it was undoubtedly a gamble to leave a staff position with Central for a freelance contract with an outfit that could fall flat on its face. History will say it very nearly did fall flat on its face, but I am happy to say it turned into an utterly exhilarating experience.

Chapter Five

MAYHEM IN THE MORNING

When the BBC broadcast their version of breakfast television for the first time on January 17th 1983, just two weeks before us, I was not alone at TVam in feeling shocked at how good it was. Compared with our efforts so far in rehearsals, Frank Bough, Selina Scott and Nick Ross had got it just right. I was demoralised because our place was in disarray. We had been working diligently on our practice runs by starting at 6am as if doing the real thing and trying to complete a real programme in real time. Sometimes, though, as we went back on problem areas over and over again, we would get to 9 o'clock and, in programme terms, we were still stuck at 6.45! Bob Hunter, brought in from ITN to head up the news operation, resigned in despair even before we went on air. I got on well with him and was sorry to see him go. It seemed to me at the time that TVam was staffed by high-flying celebrities, a sprinkling of experienced production people and then a mass of well-educated youngsters with little or no experience of television. All icing and very little cake. I had only been in television for four years, but I soon realised I was a veteran, compared with people around me. We had a staff of four hundred, of whom seventy per cent had no previous television experience. Average age 29, average salary £19,000. There were also a number of sons and daughters of famous media figures. We had Maggie Norden, daughter of Denis, James Baker, son of Richard, and Margaret Magnusson, daughter of Magnus, all members of a largely fun team to work with. Incidentally, Margaret's sister, Sally Magnusson, was working at the same time with BBC Breakfast Time. Many people fell by the wayside in those early months at TVam and I know a considerable number found it a very stressful time. All in the glare of massive national publicity, as well.

The build-up to the birth of the station was extraordinary. The presenting team and founder members soon became known as the Famous Five, after the Enid Blyton series of children's stories. Anna Ford, David Frost, Robert Kee, Michael Parkinson and Angela Rippon were all extremely well-established broadcasting figures. They were expected to dominate the early morning airwaves with their sophisticated celebrity and day one was eagerly anticipated by press and public. And all this taking part in a futuristically converted multi-storey car park in Camden in north London!

Highlight of the first morning on Tuesday, February 1st 1983, had to be John Cleese arriving in his pyjamas as the star guest. Low moment must have been an interview on female circumcision, hardly an ideal topic over the Shreddies. The decision-makers were also bold enough to foist seventeen live minutes of Norman Tebbitt onto an eager public. I presented three unerringly inconsequential sports bulletins and day one was completed. A reasonably favourable reaction from the press, but it was not long before the public gave TVam an unambiguous thumbs-down. Audiences were measured per quarter of an hour section. Figures suggested that sometimes as few as two hundred thousand were watching, although I have always had my doubts about the measuring of viewers. In those days, ratings were worked out from a survey of a mere three thousand people. Hardly representative of the whole country. Lose a hundred thousand and it probably meant five old ladies from Aberdeen had gone away on holiday.

Advertisements were few and far between and it was soon obvious that there was a burgeoning cash flow problem. Wild figures were bandied about and, at one stage, I heard we were losing as much as half a million pounds a week. A notice went up in reception saying, "Due to the current financial crisis, the light at the end of the tunnel will be turned off until further notice!"

A weatherman went away for a few days and came back to find, via his telephone messages, that he had been sacked. People were working long days, starting ferociously early and finishing late in the afternoon or even into the evening. There were some spectacular rows and I remember arguing with programme editor Hilary Lawson about the merits of sport. He did not want last night's results...only arty features on things like curling!

Peter Jay was chairman, but he resigned within weeks. I remember one of my few conversations with him. It went roughly like this.

Peter: "Ah. So you are the sports chap?"

Nick, "Yes, that's right."

Peter, "I'm a big Arsenal fan."

Nick, "Ah, well, Highbury is a magnificent stadium."

Peter, "Is it? I've never been!"

The details of the political shenanigans have been chronicled elsewhere, but suffice to say that Jonathan Aitken MP, one of the directors, took over as chairman after Peter left. This was in mid-March and, within no time, he was looking at ways of cutting costs AND improving ratings. He felt, as many did, that the current output was rather like having prawn cocktail at breakfast and people could only stomach rather more mundane fare. He needed more of a boy-next-door image and, after talks with the soon-to-be-appointed Editor-in-Chief, Greg Dyke, he approached me. I was ready, willing, reasonably able and cheap! Even before I started, he was telling me he had doubts about whether Angela and Anna were right for breakfast television, but, knowing that huge publicity was just around the corner concerning David being moved aside, I urged him to give them more time, which he did. But not much. He also asked me whom I would like to present with in a perfect world. I said Anne Diamond. "Who's she?" he asked. I explained we had worked together in the Midlands and that she was now with the BBC on Nationwide and lunchtime news bulletins.

Only a few days later, the bombshell. I received a telephone call in mid-morning from my friend, Terry Lloyd, at ITN, who later tragically died during the conflict in Iraq in 2003. We had worked together previously in the Central East newsroom in Nottingham. He asked if it was true about Anna and Angela. I had no idea what he was talking about, but he believed they had both been sacked. I soon realised he was right and the news spread around the building like a bushfire in the outback. Staff were dismayed. The whole concept of TVam was crumbling. David Frost had been replaced within eight weeks and now two more of the huge names were not only being taken off the programme, but shunted out of a job altogether.

David Frost himself had been remarkably generous to me in a time of turmoil for him. I actually first met him before the programmes went on air - in the gents. He was always great company (even in there!) and, after all the criticism he received and his subsequent removal to other projects within TVam, he was tremendously supportive. He used to come into my office for a chat, with never a hint of resentment, although I realise he must have been devastated that his project, his baby, had fallen so spectacularly flat. He was a hero of mine from the brilliant days of That Was The Week That Was when I was at school and he remained so. David had plenty to be cheerful about at the time. He had just married Carina and they were honeymooning in the United States when my appointment was announced.

Perennially upbeat, this is what he said when he arrived back at Heathrow: "To paraphrase Mark Twain, rumours of my death have been greatly exaggerated. I said, before I left, that I would be back on screen in April and so I shall – doing major interviews."

He added that there was no question of his being sacked. He would be conducting major interviews and acting as a high profile roving reporter. "As a newly-married man, the prospect of working regular hours and not having to get up at four o'clock every morning is joyous."

Finally he remarked," You will hear everything from Jonathan Aitken tomorrow. Not having to get up before dawn is fantastic and so is Nick Owen!"

It was an exciting time for me personally, but how long would the station last? With dismal ratings and pitiful income, made worse by a television commercials dispute affecting the whole industry, the prospect of fierce cost-cutting loomed large. There was a climate of dread, but somehow everyone kept going, doing the job they were being paid to do, and all this in the glare of worldwide publicity. The Famous Five were mostly well known across the world, so the TVam soap opera was big news elsewhere. We would regularly arrive for work with the forecourt in Camden packed with media, even at 4am.

We were front page news for weeks. When I was appointed, there were pictures of Jonathan and me plastered across the tabloids and broadsheets, but that was nothing compared with coverage of the dismissals of Anna and Angela. In her anger, Anna took matters into her own hands at a party and drenched Jonathan with a glass of wine. One headline in the Express reflected Michael Parkinson's view: "Bloody Shabby...Parky's fury at Anna and Angela firing." Michael had anchored some of the weekday shows, but his main job was the weekend programmes alongside his wife, Mary. There was no opposition from the BBC on Saturday or Sunday, so their ratings were far better than the weekdays, but the shows were good anyway. Michael said that he was now considering his future, after the sackings of Anna and Angela. Michael and I often used to pop across the road for a pint at the Devonshire Arms in Hawley Crescent. What a boost it was for the beleaguered workforce to see Parky stroll in!

Anna and Angela, of course, were and still are two of the best-known women presenters in British television. It was a pleasure to meet them in the first place and I felt privileged to work alongside them. It is no surprise that their demise caused such uproar. Officially, they were said to have lost their jobs because they had breached their contracts by speaking out over the departure of Peter Jay. TV Mayhem was the new name for the company in the press...Britain's number one soap opera!

Angela had been particularly kind to me before the volcanic events of April. She took me to one side after the first few weeks on air to say I was highly rated by the management and had a great future at TVam. Even so, I think it was a distinct shock to her system when I was propelled into the seat alongside her on the sofa. She visibly cooled towards me, but was never unpleasant to my face, though she did remark after the first hour of my first programme, "It's not as easy as you think, is it?" Those allegedly in-the-know told me she thought I was far too wet behind the ears for a main presenting role, but we only had four days together before Anna took over and Angela went away for a break and some work in Australia.

Nothing could have prepared Angela for the 24 hours at the end of her trip and her arrival back in Britain. She learned she was to come off presenting for the time being and that viewers had precipitated the decision because of her manner on the programme towards me. The News of the World had a page lead, which I later found out came from an insider at TVam with an axe to grind. The headline said, "Angela Upsets New Boy Nick" and claimed angry viewers forced the sacking of Angela from her star role on breakfast TV because they complained she was nasty to new-boy presenter Nick Owen. It said bosses were alarmed at the number of calls about Angela's sideswipes. It showed a picture of me with the caption, "Nick: in despair." Well, I was certainly not in despair, far from it. It was never going to be a partnership made in heaven, but much of the banter was just that...edgy cut-and-thrust with a fellow professional, something I indulge in on my current programme, BBC Midlands Today, and have done in virtually all the live television I have presented over more than a quarter of a century. It is my style, more so with every passing year, although I was asked only a few months down the line to cut back on my digs at Wincey Willis at the weather board because they were a bit over the top. We are very close friends and she loved it. In fact, she gave every bit as good as she got. More on wonderful Wincey later.

The News of the World article about Angela threw in words such as patronising, haughty, beastly, unfriendly and even monster. It must have been shattering for her and I am not surprised she became so angry about it. After she left TVam, I wrote to her saying how sorry I was at the turn of events and emphasising that I had no part in that vicious article. Truth is that the first I knew about it was when I received a call from my local newsagent saying I had better come down and buy a copy! No, the knives were definitely out for Angela somewhere in the hierarchy and that has to be the source. After my letter, she sent a cordial reply and wished me the best of luck for the future. We bump into each other occasionally and I hope there is no major problem, although I am sure she associates me with the most traumatic time of her professional life. However, let me just remind you that we only presented together for four days, twelve hours.....surely that could not have played any substantial part in deciding her future at TVam?

At the news conference to announce the arrival of Greg Dyke and my promotion to main male presenter, I had described myself as an ordinary guy. That was in answer to the tricky question of what did I have that David Frost didn't. What else could I say? I had neither the profile nor the experience of David, but I believed I was a good presenter, with a solid grounding in journalism, plus a common touch, if that does not sound patronising. I wanted to be the boy-next-door whom you would talk to over the garden fence, speaking the same language. It gave the press some easy ammunition to take the mickey. I soon became Mr. Ordinary in a mostly derogatory way, but I was hardly likely to stand on the rooftops and shout "Hey look at me I am the f***ing greatest" was I?

On the demise of Anna and Angela, Clive Jones was now running the show before the advent of Greg Dyke. Clive and I had not seen each other for more than ten years since we worked together as graduate trainees at the Doncaster Evening Post. We had always been mates there, but he was married with children comparatively young, so his social life was somewhat more sedate than mine! His marriage broke up after he left Doncaster and he later made headlines when he married TV presenter Fern Britton. Sadly, that marriage too came to an end, but Clive's career has been one upward climb. Amongst his many senior posts, he became Chief Executive of Carlton Television and Chief Executive of ITV News. He was fairly highly placed in the beginning at TVam and had interviewed me for the sports job, but now after various resignations and sackings at management level, he was editor for the time being and decided to introduce a new presenter to join me on the sofa.

Lynda Berry was another old friend and colleague. We had both worked together in the newsroom at ATV before she went south to TVS. She was very attractive with a great sense of humour and I was delighted when we teamed up again. She was already working at TVam as a reporter and newsreader and had rightly distinguished herself with some royal reports for the programme from Australia. Lynda seemed to me to be very anxious on air and, although she had an extremely pleasant manner about her, Greg made a decision on his first day at the end of April that she was not the right person to take us forward. He asked me about Anne Diamond because Jonathan had told him about our conversation at the beginning of the month and he wondered if I could arrange a meeting. I did, they saw each other in a pub that night and she eventually agreed to sign on for TVam. Lynda duly heard rumours emanating from Birmingham, where all three of us had worked together, and decided never to speak to me again…unless she had to. We did, of course, have conversations on air, but that was it. She never spoke to me on any other occasion. Not once. We shared an office, but when I walked in at about 4 am she would walk out and sit somewhere else! She was never too crazy about Anne from their early days in the Midlands, so she did not talk to her either after she arrived at TVam.

To facilitate the contractual side of Anne's leaving the BBC, she needed outside help and I recommended my agent, Paul Vaughan. The relationship worked for only a short time. They fell out with dreadful bitterness and this led ultimately to an acrimonious court case, which cost Anne hundreds of thousands of pounds and prompted me to leave Paul's agency. That was still some years in the future..for now, Anne was having to work her notice at the BBC and Greg was busy devising a relaunch.

He felt strongly that the station's output was far too narrow, catering only for the chattering classes in Hampstead, so his first target was to broaden the content, make it more accessible to more people and lift the profile by introducing some glitzy names. He said at the time, "The programme needs to be funnier, more human, more relaxed." On the day his and my appointments were announced the BBC's average peak audience was 1.8 million, we were getting 400,000.

Greg brought in a number of excellent producer-directors such as Bob Collins, John McColgan and Bob Merrilees, but his first in-front-of-camera signing was Wincey Willis and what a stroke of inspiration that was.

Greg had spotted Wincey presenting the weather in her native north-east for Tyne Tees Television. She was the pioneer of the skittish, fun weather presenter who played an integral part in a programme….a broadcaster first, weather person second. You might remember Barbara Edwards. She was the first woman to deliver weather forecasts for the BBC in the seventies, but that was long before meteorologists were able to show a personality of their own. It was purely a straight forecast with no frills. Even so, it was still high profile and Barbara gave up after four years in the public eye because she became disillusioned with constant criticism of the way she dressed, something that was never a problem for her male colleagues. So Wincey was really a first of her kind and she took over the weather role five days a week, replacing the plummy tones of Commander David Philpott who had built up a following of his own with his patrician naval bearing. David moved to the weekends.

Wincey made her first appearance on relaunch day, May 23rd, 1983. TVam had been on air a mere sixteen weeks and it had already torn up the script and started again! Also, making her television entrance on that pivotal day was Lizzie Webb, or Mad Lizzie as she became known. Greg was keen to have a fun, keep-fit slot, but felt it had been a little too serious under the previous regime, no pain, no gain and so on. Greg's PA Jane Tatnall used to attend Lizzie's fitness classes, Greg met up with her and she joined the payroll. Another excellent addition to the team which helped us rocket up the ratings and ultimately force the BBC into its own relaunch. At this stage, our peak audience in any quarter of an hour period was about 400,000, compared with the BBC's 1,700,000. In other words, their figures were estimated to be at least four times greater than ours.

The guests Lynda and I interviewed on that relaunch day included politician Cecil Parkinson, comedian Lennie Bennett and boxing giant, Henry Cooper. Peter Cushing joined us that week, as did Del Shannon, Jilly Cooper, Kathy Kirby, Lulu, Demis Roussos, Bernie Winters and a certain Jimmy Greaves, who became another regular member of Greg's new strike force. Not a bad cast list for a television station that was being mocked mercilessly in the press and had to suffer a fair number of snubs from potential guests who turned us down because of our poor image. How it was all going to change!

Anne joined on D-Day, June 6th, 1983, and for our first morning together on national TV, we entertained, amongst others, political heavyweights Ted Heath and Denis Healey, comedian Dickie Henderson and Uri Geller. Also in that week, we had Howard and Blair on the same show. Michael and Lionel! Thursday of that debut week for Anne was General Election day and, on the following morning, I shaped up for the first of many sparring sessions with the most pugnacious union leader of the time, Arthur Scargill.

It was marvellous to be working in partnership with Anne again after our abortive attempts to front Central News in Nottingham and, as our bright new team began to emerge, the tide of publicity turned. There were a number of critical moments that made us think there were happier times ahead, although we were still well behind in the ratings.

David Essex appeared as a guest both for us and the BBC's Breakfast Time, but later he was invited to take part in Ludovic Kennedy's Did You See show, a BBC2 review of television programmes. That particular week they were looking at the merits of breakfast television. Newspaper critic Gillian Reynolds said, oh so humorously, that she was thinking of suing the BBC for brain damage after a week of having to watch TVam. David analysed both shows and was then asked, if he had a choice of going back, which he would choose. He replied, "TVam with Anne and Nick, because it's warmer." It was just about the first time anyone had said anything remotely pleasant about us and meant a lot. I have spent many hours with David since and I often remind him of that remark. Simple as it may seem now, it gave us a lot of encouragement at a time when we felt besieged.

Chris Tarrant joined us in mid-summer, a man in limbo after his success with Tiswas, on the one hand, and then the axeing of his OTT Saturday night show, on the other. It was probably far too daring and raunchy for its time, even though it aired late at night. Greg hired him to front a series of outside broadcasts from beaches around Britain with his own brand of wacky humour. The first outing was to be 6.50am on Blackpool beach and, with our ratings still allegedly fairly low, we wondered whether anyone would know he was going to be there, let alone turn up at such an ungodly hour. To our astonishment, an estimated three thousand people rolled up for the fun and the numbers grew with every passing minute. I still smile at the memory of Chris stuffing a live ferret down his trousers on one of those mornings. For weeks afterwards, as he chose to wear fairly tight fitting pants, we were often convinced the ferret was still there. Chris was a huge hit all around the country; again it vastly improved our profile and ratings and Chris was offered a little job as a disc jockey for Capital Radio in London as a result. He hesitated for a while because he feared it was only local radio, but, wow, did it revitalise his career!

Thursday, August 25th, was pivotal too. We had our first international superstar pop band on the show and the reaction to their appearance really made us feel we were getting somewhere. Barry, Maurice and Robin Gibb of the Bee Gees joined us at eight o'clock and proceeded to light up the place with their banter and anecdotes. It was mesmerising. Office staff came to work early to snatch a glimpse, guests who had finished the sport stayed on and we dropped scheduled items to give the Bee Gees as much time as possible. Anne and I enjoyed it so much that we almost forgot we were presenting a television programme. What made it stand out in the memory that little bit more is the number of letters and phone calls we received over the next few days. They all said how much the viewers enjoyed it, but a considerable number told us how they had been late for work or school, because they had held on until 9.25 am, the very end of the programme.

Roland Rat was really catching on by mid-summer. He had first been introduced by the head of children's programmes, Anne Wood, round about Easter when Anna and Angela were still at TVam. This was before Greg arrived, so it is a myth that he unleashed that insolent, irreverent puppet onto the world. What he did do, though, was to spot his potential, so he made the best of him. He put him on as much as possible during school holidays and sent him abroad for specials. As the children grew more and more infatuated, so their parents following up behind realised that there was some quite decent stuff coming out of the rest of TVam's output. Roland, in the person of David Claridge, was very funny indeed, though I must say it was never easy bantering with a lump of cloth when the real voice was coming from David lying at our feet! He called me Nickelarse and told Anne he had seen better looking birds on the check-out at Tesco!

One of Greg Dyke's greatest coups to lift our profile to the stratosphere had to be the signing of Diana Dors. The ultimate Hollywood-type blonde bombshell, Britain's answer to Marilyn Monroe, Diana was loved by millions in the fifties and sixties and hugely admired as she developed into a talented character actress in her later years. She was suffering poor health when she joined us and the drugs she was taking to fight her ovarian cancer had played havoc with her weight. It was agreed that she would do a regular weekly spot with us about a healthy diet and the eternal battle with her waistline. It was my task to see how she was responding to the new healthy recipes she was recommending. With the help of home economist Carol Bowen, Diana used to talk me through the ingredients every Friday and then I would put her on the scales. Remarkably, she dropped a few pounds every time. We were all really proud of her. It was only much later that she revealed she had initially filled her pockets with lead weights the first time around and gradually reduced the load every succeeding Friday!

Because of her well-documented pastime of living life to the full, Diana was also a popular choice to be an agony aunt for us after the weight-watching series. People loved writing to her or coming through to her live on the telephone, but it was not always easy for me to keep a straight face because of the chat I was getting in my ear from the director. Approaching Guy Fawkes night one time, Diana was warning people of the dangers of fireworks and recalling a disastrous party she had attended when she lived in Hollywood. A man had died of a heart attack, the house had caught fire and these were only a few of the mishaps that ruined what should have been a glittering extravaganza. Irish director Bob Collins came through on talk-back, "Don't ever invite me to a party with you, Diana," he said. I could see the camera crew weeping with laughter as they tried to contain themselves in a live studio.

Another time, a viewer had written in with a horrendous tale of woe. It seemed a never ending catalogue of illness, injury and infidelity, benighting a poor woman's wretched life. "Diana, what on earth do you think I should do?" she asked. "Ever thought of suicide?" said Bob Collins helpfully down talkback. Again, presenter and crew beside themselves.

I visited Diana's home in Surrey and toured the place open-mouthed. Thick white carpets which required all visitors to take off their shoes in the kitchen, a swimming pool that formed an integral part of the living room, the biggest television screen I had ever seen and CCTV all around the grounds, something I had never come across all that time ago. She and her husband Alan Lake became my good friends in the short time I knew them. I used to spend as much time as I could chatting to them on their weekly visits to Camden. Tragically, Diana succumbed to her ovarian cancer in May 1984 and Alan, unable to cope without her, shot himself not long afterwards. Diana's successor as grande dame and mother confessor at TVam was Pat Phoenix, of Elsie Tanner fame in Coronation Street. By a sad irony, she also lost her life to cancer some two years after Diana. She too had become a popular member of the team and, like Diana, a valued friend. I still treasure a rare and exotic jug she gave Jill and me one Christmas.

Anne, Wincey and I attended Diana's funeral in Sunningdale in Berkshire in the company of some huge showbiz stars and one of the notorious Krays, Reggie, slipped in at the back, handcuffed to a detective. Diana knew and was loved by admirers from all walks of life. Among the mourners that day was Freddie Starr, who had previously come to the studio immediately after she died to talk about Diana and his friendship with her. The first thing he did was give me a big kiss on the lips! He wanted to apologise for his last appearance on the programme when he had been frankly almost impossible to interview. Nearly every question had received a one-word answer and there was a constant feeling of impending disaster. Not a comfortable morning at all. On this latest occasion, he explained that he had been heavily under the influence of Valium and he really had no clue what he was doing. Obviously, I have seen Freddie interviewed many times since on television and sympathised as the presenters have squirmed in the atmosphere of imminent mischief. He is compulsive viewing, though, and brilliantly entertaining on stage.

Freddie is not the only guest who brings the word 'danger' emblazoned on his forehead. I interviewed Oliver Reed a couple of times and he was never sober! The first time was at TVam when he had been up drinking and playing cards all night at his hotel nearby. He lurched into the studio, plonked himself down and somehow managed to conduct a conversation with Anne and me, despite the fact his eyes seemed to be focused on some distant planet, after at least 24 hours with no sleep. He had that familiar look of brooding menace, which gave him such presence on the screen. We interviewed Oliver once more some ten years later on Good Morning with Anne and Nick and, yet again, he was out of it. He took to the studio floor with a can of lager in his hand and again we somehow muddled through. The most enduring memory of Oliver Reed, I suppose, is the time he staggered around on Michael Aspel's show. Faintly amusing, mildly embarrassing and, overall, very sad. I worked with his brother, Simon Reed, for many years on ITV Sport. A top bloke, who looked very like Oliver, but I could never quite come to terms with the fact that they were brothers, because they were so different as individuals.

On the subject of booze, it has long grieved me the way things have turned out for George Best. I have seen Pele and Maradona in the flesh, but, for me, George will always be the finest footballer that lived. I have interviewed him countless times and downed the odd tincture at the bar with him, but still had to go along with the painful decision, made by producer Trevor East, to turn him away from one of our ITV Midweek Sport Special programmes in the late eighties. He was well away when he appeared on Wogan earlier in the evening and, when he staggered through our revolving doors at the Thames TV studios in Euston Road shortly afterwards, it was clearly hopeless. Fancy having to turn away George Best from a guest spot on your sports show! There was no option really and I have no doubt, if he had come on the show, it would have been excruciating. Besides his sporting genius, he is an utterly charismatic individual. It makes it all the more difficult to reconcile where he is now with what he once was. As a football fan, I feel cheated that we were deprived of another ten years of Best at his finest on the football field.

I have jumped ahead. Back in the summer of 1983, TVam was beginning to take off. The ratings were rising steadily and I can still picture where I was when I heard we had passed the one million mark. I was having a family holiday near Falmouth in Cornwall and Martin Wainwright, a Guardian writer and contemporary of mine at school, was standing in alongside Anne. I rang the office from a phone box to

*The bride wore khaki. Esme and Bertie on their Wedding Day –
October 22nd, 1945.*

Learning how to face the camera. Mother, father and me, age about 2.

Young sports reporter interviewing young Aston Villa footballer (later Manager) John Gregory.

Early days at BBC Radio Birmingham.

Learning how to pose for camera when still on radio. Note stylish leather jacket and tidy hair.

A boy in a man's world! Early days in journalism as a reporter on
The Birmingham Post (1972).

Negotiating with WBA Manager Ron Atkinson.

Freezing on the touchline with friend Graham Clarke in Poland during Aston Villa's UEFA Cup run. Bitter row later that night with Ron Saunders.

Showing a neat line in shirts during early days in broadcasting at BBC Radio Birmingham.

Same night as above opposite in Katowice!

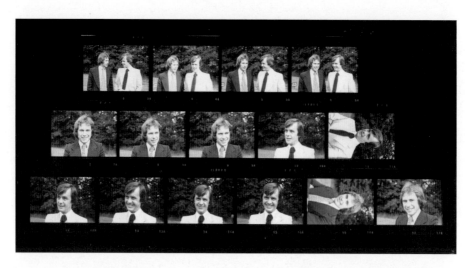

*First steps in TV. Publicity shots by Charlie Moody, before my one off sports
programme for BBC Midlands in the Summer of 1977 (co-pres. Peter Windows).*

*ATV Sports Team photo. Includes 3rd and 4th from left Trevor East and me,
6th left Jimmy Greaves, then Gary Newbon, Billy Wright and John Dickinson.
Fishing guru, Terry Thomas, extreme left.*

ATV All Stars football team. Jasper at back. Middle row includes Jim Smith (manager of Birmingham at time), Bev Bevan next to him then Robert Plant, Gary Newbon 2nd from right, Don Maclean 3rd from right. N.O. left front row. Trevor East 3rd left.

Did I really need a police escort? On duty at W.B.A.'s ground, the Hawthorns.

Wedding Day 1977.

Another illustration of my immaculate taste in shirts.

Anne Diamond, Nick Owen, Wincey Willis

The trio that enjoyed such happy and successful times at TVam – Anne, me, Wincey.

How the team grew at TVam. Left to right: Jayne Irving, Gordon Honeycombe, Lizzie Webb, me, Anne D, Roland Rat, John Stapleton, Wincey Willis and sports presenter Mike Morris.

Lucky man or what? With Jayne Irving, Anne D, Wincey Willis and Mad Lizzie Webb at TVam.

*Degree in Classics, qualified in journalism, it came to this – talking to a rat!
We had some fantastic laughs!*

With Joanna Lumley shortly after I had asked her if she was wearing knickers.

A regular and popular guest at breakfast – former P.M. Ted Heath.

Rare moments at home with Jill and Oedipus.

One of our many encounters with Elton John.

Celebrating Adam Faith as Elton worries about his room bill at the Savoy.

Pamela Stephenson gets a hold of me. If only she had tried in private!

say hello and was told the happy news. So I was in happy mood as I drove the family home and then headed on to a party in the Sussex countryside at the magnificent home of Timothy Aitken, Jonathan's cousin and now chief executive of TVam. It was there that I had my first proper meeting with royalty. I did not realise it then but it was to lead to an interview that was apparently seen by 500 million people in 141 countries around the world.

Chapter Six

PROBING A PRINCESS

Tim Aitken's Saturday night party in the grounds of his splendid home in East Sussex held an intriguing mix of showbusiness personalities and city high flyers. On arrival, I met up with Wincey, who told me Greg Dyke had signed up a new male presenter, while I was away on holiday, John Stapleton from BBC Nationwide. She said she and Anne had gone in to see Greg in my absence to ask why John had been brought in...was Nick's job under threat, or anyone else's for that matter? I was not particularly worried myself and it soon became clear that John's remit was to focus on one heavy interview a day from the major story of the moment and to act as a stand-in for Anne and me. We became close friends very quickly and I am glad to say there was never a hint of rivalry. Even so, John still recalls his first meeting with Anne after he arrived. He says she looked daggers at him and asked, "Why are you here?"

As it turned out, John and I regularly co-presented one show a week when Anne took time off and one of the best mornings we spent together came in April 1984, when Eric Morecambe joined us for an hour and a half on the sofa. More of that later, but suffice to say now that John became a very popular part of the team, another vital ingredient in Greg's recipe that ultimately made TVam the most profitable television station in the world.

I stayed the night at Tim's as did Prince and Princess Michael of Kent. Prince Michael worked as a business partner of the Aitken cousins, so I had already met the royal couple on previous social occasions. It was strange to be sitting with them at breakfast, Princess Michael in her dressing gown and her husband spruced and ready to head off for a day's carriage racing in Windsor. It was intriguing to watch Princess Michael trawling through the Sunday newspapers, passing comment on the mountain of royal gossip. She was great company and very amusing.

So it was that we had developed a more than passing acquaintance, when a headline story broke in April 1985 that Princess Michael's father, Baron Von Reibnitz, had been a member of Hitler's dreaded SS. The Daily Mirror's Royal Correspondent, James Whitaker, got the exclusive and he appeared on our programme that morning to back up the newspaper's claim that there had been a cover-up. It was a sensational story and a genuine scoop for James and the Mirror.

After the show, my private thoughts were largely directed towards the evening, when I was planning to watch my team Luton Town play a vital relegation match against Norwich in the old First Division. Little did I know that the next twenty four hours would be quite so dramatic and that I would not have a hope of getting to the game!

Unknown to me, Timothy Aitken was putting the idea to Princess Michael of talking to us about the claims concerning her father. In those days, it was unheard of for a member of the royal family to give an interview on anything but a favourite charity. Surely a so-called hard news interview would be out of the question? Well, it was not dismissed out of hand, so Timothy felt optimistic enough mid-morning to warn me that I might have to miss my football match. The Princess, meanwhile, was being bombarded with advice NOT to be interviewed, but she was bursting to give an honest account of her position and I gather, significantly, that just one person said, "Go ahead, if you want to." Her Majesty the Queen.

I left the office for my Kentish Town flat at lunchtime, because I would need a quick sleep, whether I was off to Kenilworth Road or Kensington Palace. Either way, I would be heading for the Kenny! I had been deeply asleep for about fifteen minutes when the phone rang and the gruff northern voice of our head of news, Bill Ludford, told me, "Football's off, lad. You're off to t'Palace!"

So it was out with the best suit, a quick bath and back to the office within twenty minutes to prepare. I talked with Bill about how hard I could be…after all, as I said earlier, this sort of situation was so unusual it was slightly difficult knowing how to approach it. We agreed that it had to be treated like any other interview, otherwise it would have appeared like a party political broadcast for Princess Michael. I sat alone jotting down the questions I wanted to ask before I was joined by the crew going with me, Stuart, Richard and Ian. They had enough equipment to film a sequel to Ben Hur, but we had to be sure there would be no technical failures. We kept in almost constant touch with the office by radio telephone on the way there – mobiles had not yet been invented – and had to recite a set line every time we passed a police checkpoint, as we approached the Palace. We swept pass the press corps, doorstepping some considerable distance from the Palace itself, and cruised up the drive to the door.

Besides the Palace aides, we were met by Tim Aitken himself, looking more boyish than ever, sporting an anxious smile, but confident that TVam was onto its biggest coup since we went on air two years before. He led me straight into Princess Michael's plush study and she rushed over with a warm, "Hello, Nick, how are you?" I replied, "More importantly, how are you?" She did not hesitate, "Absolutely rotten!"

A stunning-looking lady, but her eyes gave away the stress she was under and I learned later that she had been reduced to tears more than once since the story broke. She left us alone as the crew set up and I told Tim how I planned to conduct the interview. He never once told me what to ask, despite the assertion of a crassly-ill-informed Observer columnist who claimed that Tim wrote the questions. Rubbish.

I asked for the loo while I was there and they should have given me a map, because I twice got lost in the corridors. I finally entered a room with a washbasin, but no sign of the crucial apparatus I sought. I then noticed a beautiful antique chair in the corner had a mysterious wooden box suspended above it, whence hung a chain. Ah! I was intrigued by the pile of magazines alongside the loo and the joke books. Some highly irreverent stuff!

The interview itself went smoothly enough and I was convinced that Princess Michael was telling the truth when she said she had no idea her father had been an officer in the SS. She claimed that her mother had deliberately kept the information from her, but, anyway, evidence was on its way from Germany to say he had been completely exonerated of any crimes after the war by the Allies. She also said she had found out since the newspaper revelations that he had only held an honorary rank in the SS and that he had been expelled from the party for his anti-Nazi views. In fact, he was punished by being sent to the eastern front.

At one stage, I asked her, "Are you ashamed, embarrassed, upset, devastated?"

She replied, "I was desperately ashamed at first and then, when I spoke to my brother, he explained to me the document which exonerated my father from any activity which I have been brought up to believe that the SS meant... one thing, basically concentration camps for Jews and so on. I have now discovered that he was not involved with anything like that at all, so I am relieved to have discovered that. But, yes, it is a deep shame for me."

She told me she could well understand people's reaction of horror, but she wanted to stress that there had also been considerable false speculation. I pointed out to her that an Australian writer had alleged her father had the say-so on whether people went into or came out of concentration camps. She dismissed that as one of many fairy stories written about her and she stressed that she had received messages of support from the royal family.

I wondered how she would feel when she next performed a public duty. She replied, "I don't know what I shall feel. I just think when dreadful things come to you out of the blue, you have to live with them. I mean, it is like suddenly discovering that you are adopted. Here I am forty years old and I suddenly discover something that is quite unpleasant and I shall just simply have to live with it. What the public's perception of me will be I don't know. I wasn't alive when all this happened, so I hope they will judge me on my own performance and what I am and what I stand for."

Would she feel slight resentment that people were visiting the sins of a father on the daughter?

"No, I think it is perfectly natural. Maybe that would be my reaction too. No, I don't feel resentment – I understand. I don't like it, but I understand it."

I rounded up with this final question, "What has it been like for you, the last thirty six hours or so?"

The princess, "I think I have been in a sort of state of shellshock, but it is something I will have to come to terms with and I know I shall. I don't like it, but I will have to live with it."

As we packed our equipment away in the late afternoon, the Prince arrived home, not even knowing the interview had taken place. He watched the playback and seemed reasonably happy, but there was clearly a question mark over whether he and the Princess would allow it to be broadcast. What swung it, ironically, was the BBC's Six O'Clock news, which they believed was vindictive and inaccurate, implying that Baron Von Reibnitz could have been responsible for all manner of horrors. After watching that, Prince and Princess Michael knew their side of the story had to be heard.

I left Kensington Palace in Tim Aitken's sporty little BMW, along with journalist colleague Peter Van Gelder, and we were all excited that we had landed a spectacular interview. Judging by world reaction the next day, we had.

Tory MP Anthony Beaumont-Dark, on the programme the next day, described it as the most remarkable interview he had ever seen, adding, "I have a hunch that her popularity rating, instead of going down, will now go up."

Daily Mail columnist Nigel Dempster was another guest on the show that morning, April 17th, 1985. He cringed at my question about her being embarrassed or ashamed. "How did you dare ask that?" he said. How things have changed in our approach to royalty in the years since, but, at the time, I had been concerned to ask the delicate questions gently, but still make sure they were asked. I was after a balance between the over-aggressive and the too soft.

After row upon row overnight with our newsdesk over whether they could have the interview, the BBC ultimately lifted the lot and played it out a number of times on Breakfast Time. They got into trouble for it from TVam's lawyers and had to fork out a tidy sum to make up for it. Interestingly, the BBC's producer on duty, Maurice Blisson, tells me they were contacted by the Palace and encouraged to show it. They recorded it off transmission and replayed it with a blank strip covering our "exclusive" logo.

We broadcast about eight and a half minutes every half an hour on TVam that morning and soon it was being show around the world. Shortly afterwards I visited the United States. I even had people coming up to me out-of-the-blue over there to say they had seen the piece.

I was swamped with letters, most notably perhaps from the then Controller of BBC 1, Michael Grade, which, I must say, surprised and delighted me. He said, "Well played. A super interview with the Princess. Right tone, right questions, in the right order! Congratulations to you, Yours, Michael Grade." A lesser mortal in a BBC newsroom signed himself 'a fellow toiler in the vineyard' and pointed out that he had once thought of me as a wimp, but had now changed his mind. "You asked all the questions which many would have funked," he wrote. The letters were mostly very enthusiastic, but some of the extreme views from the letters were quite staggering. One suggested sending a bucket of whitewash to help finish the job of 'clearing' the Princess, but others chastised my cruel questioning of an innocent lady. I must quote from one I received from Wrexham, which I thought was a masterpiece.

"The reputation of the media in this country is and always has been low. ...yet even in this intellectual sewer, you managed to plumb new depths.....your interrogation of Princess Michael filled me with indignation. I wish you could have seen yourself through ordinary eyes. The phoney indignation, the contrived moral superiority, the patronising impudence of the slimy little bully, backed up by the gang. In you, I could see the poodle yapping at the tethered wolfhound."

I also heard from the journalist who had started the whole furore. James Whitaker had been on our sofa on the morning his story broke and he had obviously watched Princess Michael's reply with enormous interest. He told me, "Your interview with HRH was superb. Many congratulations." He had come in for considerable criticism from some quarters merely for revealing the story in the first place and for the tone of the Mirror's editorial on the same day. He said, "It is at such moments I have to force myself to follow Queen Victoria's excellent advice. Never complain. Never explain."

I saw the Princess a few times after that. She officially opened a new school attended by my children in Berkhamsted in the November of 1985 and enchanted everyone she met. She created huge excitement as her helicopter thundered into the beautiful, rural grounds of Haresfoot School for the ceremony, but caused great consternation a few weeks earlier when she phoned me at home and got the babysitter. The young girl thought it was a wind-up. Then it dawned on her that she really was talking to royalty, she nearly collapsed and never babysat for us again!

Chapter Seven

GRAB HIS GOOLIES!

I know I am not alone in regarding Eric Morecambe as the greatest comedian of all time. Like Tommy Cooper, he had the ability to make you laugh just by entering the room, but Eric had an extra ingredient for me, his love of football and, in particular, Luton Town, the team I had supported since I was ten years old. Every passing reference to Luton on the Morecambe and Wise shows was a marvellous boost for a small town club such as ours, so I was thrilled when I learned he was to be our guest on Good Morning Britain on TVam in April 1984. John Stapleton and I were the presenters and I look back now with mixed emotions on what I regard as my most memorable morning on breakfast television.

Eric greeted me with the customary handshake that never was, as his proffered hand shot to his glasses to leave me floundering and I then passed him a cup of tea in a Luton mug. I had been to Luton's match the night before at West Ham and specially saved him a programme. I handed it over, in the forlorn hope he would be delighted.

"Thanks very much," he said. "I shall treasure that." And promptly threw it over his shoulder! The floor crew were beginning to lose it!

We showed an hilarious sketch, which featured Sir Ralph Richardson, and Eric explained how hard it was for serious, straight actors to feel at home in a Morecambe and Wise setting. He told us, "Sir Ralph didn't enjoy it very much. He said he felt like a cat who'd been thrown out of the back door in the middle of a storm."

We included one of Glenda Jackson's famous contributions to the Morecambe and Wise show – "she only got one pound for that" – and Eric pointed out that Peter Cushing was the first big name to 'submit'. "Then he bit my neck and left."

He talked lovingly about his wife Joan, adding, "We have three children, though it may be four now. I haven't been home for a week!"

We gave him a birthday card to read out which went on and on. "Please say happy birthday to my grandma on the fifteenth; my grandfather on the twenty ninth; my mum Linda on the seventeenth; my friend Lorraine on the sixteenth; Jennifer on the eighteenth; Barry on the thirtieth...I've picked a right one here, "Eric shouted. "I watch you every morning. THINK you!" Fifteen minutes later, after the news, weather from Wincey and a separate item, we returned to Eric mumbling on, "...and Auntie Rose. Happy birthday to Uncle Fred, cousin Marvin, good luck with the wedding, hope the baby enjoys it...great novel this!"

He did not talk seriously that much, but he did admit that he found the news generally fairly depressing. Perhaps not very original, but he wished there could be a five minute good news spot every morning on a programme such as ours.

"Thanks for the moment," said John Stapleton. "Can you stay with us for a while longer?"

"Stay with you? I could marry you," Eric replied.

In the closing stages of the programme, after he had been with us for well over an hour, he talked about his health, even then adding a touch of humour. "My heart's very good, it just stops for half an hour a day."

"My (by-pass) operation was five years ago and, before it, I was given just three months to live. I get loads of letters, telling of relatives who are terrified of an operation, "Eric told us. "I write and encourage them. It's a marvellous operation." He certainly looked a good advertisement for heart surgery. He was on top of the world and seemed fit and tanned.

He stayed with us for another hour and a half after the show and joined us for breakfast in the TVam canteen by the waterside at Camden Lock. A party of schoolchildren was being shown round the building and he enchanted every one of them. He signed all their autographs, as you would hope, but what struck me is that he had a separate word and joke with each individual child and there must have been at least twenty of them. I do hope they were old enough then to have that treasured memory now of a very special man.

So Eric left a marvellously warm glow behind him as he left TVam that sunny April morning. Bearing in mind his apparently vibrant good health, it's shattering to think that a mere forty days later dear Eric was dead. And the way I found out about it is rather bizarre.

Ernie Wise, Eric's partner of forty years, was due to be a guest on TVam on the morning of May 29th, 1984. I had a day off that day, so when I tuned in at home I was fully expecting to see Anne and John with Ernie on the sofa shortly after eight o'clock. However, I switched on at ten past seven and Ernie was already on, being interviewed alone by John. I thought it odd and slowly it dawned on me that Ernie was dressed in black and talking about Eric in the past tense. Of course, it soon emerged that Eric had died overnight of a heart attack which occurred after he had performed in a charity concert at Tewkesbury in Gloucestershire. He was only 58. How brave it was of Ernie to honour his commitment that day to appear live on our programme and what a strange coincidence it was from our point of view that he was booked to be with us. Naturally, he would have been the first person we would have invited on anyway in the light of the tragic events in Gloucestershire.

I feel privileged to have known Eric just a little and to have conducted what may well have been his last television interview. I had great affection too for Ernie…I interviewed him many times and chatted to him at countless social events. He lived for another fifteen years after losing his partner and died in March 1999, aged 73.

It is always a joy interviewing comedians and, besides Eric and Ernie, I have been lucky enough to talk to many of the best since I came into television, including Jasper Carrott, Bob Monkhouse, Frankie Howerd, Les Dawson and Bob Hope in his back garden in Los Angeles. I remember a remarkable pairing too! We had Kenneth Williams and Bernard Manning sitting alongside each other one morning – some contrast in style! At one stage, Manning said to Williams, "You're so bloody unlucky, if you fell into a barrel load of tits, you'd come out sucking your thumb." Racy stuff at breakfast time in the early eighties!

My encounter with then-comedienne Pamela Stephenson of Not The Nine O'Clock News fame was so riotous it must be in my medical notes somewhere. She starred in that brilliant satirical series that first brought to our notice the likes of Rowan Atkinson, Mel Smith and Griff Rhys-Jones. She came to us in November 1985 to tell us about her forthcoming one-woman tour and she certainly achieved maximum publicity after trying to rip my trousers off. It so happened that I had recently had a minor operation on a slipped disc in my back, so I was wearing a zip-up plaster cast round my middle and feeling fairly fragile. A book had recently come out suggesting I was one of the less interesting people in Britain because of that business about being just an ordinary guy. Pamela suddenly took it upon herself to illuminate my image by shouting, "Grab his goolies!" She pulled down my zip and wrestled with my belt. Anne was non-plussed and had a small cushion, very small actually, on standby to cover my credentials, should the need arise. Pamela was also trying to stuff coloured gel into my hair and I was desperately trying to fight her off. The jostling seemed to carry on for a good minute or so before she revealed I was wearing striped underpants. Then she gave up and sat down again. The crew and the rest of my colleagues loved it and I am sure it was very amusing to watch, but I was more concerned with the damage it was doing to my bad back.

The incident caused uproar in the building, viewers called in their hundreds to complain and the press calls started almost immediately. Our press office wanted to re-create the incident for photographs, so somewhat gingerly I agreed and the two of us returned to the sofa half an hour afterwards. The pictures hit most of the tabloids. The incident itself was shown on countless blooper-type programmes afterwards until Pamela put a block on it, presumably because she felt that the comedic side of her life was over and she had moved on to a more cerebral life as a doctor of psychology in the United States.

One of the first television cooks, Fanny Cradock, was a fellow guest on the show that day and the grand old lady was clearly taken aback by the turn of events. She was a fairly intimidating woman who had famously worked alongside husband Johnny in her television kitchen. She always gave him a hard time on air, but, as far as posterity goes, it strikes me he had the last word. Fanny was famously cooking doughnuts once and they did not come out of the oven as planned. Johnny wrapped up that particular show with the immortal words to their viewers, "And let's hope your doughnuts don't end up looking like Fanny's!" Fanny was so infuriated by Pamela's antics that she wrote a letter to me afterwards. In it, she expressed her dismay, berated Pamela, sympathised with my predicament on a live show and hoped it had not caused too much damage to my back.

Sadly, it had caused havoc to my back and things were hardly improved by my making a hurried trip to Scotland the next day. That came about because I had made a chance remark on that same Pamela Stephenson show that I had never been north of Hadrian's Wall. The Scottish Tourist Board were on the phone in no time and, within twenty four hours, I was whisked up to Glasgow to be greeted by a wee lassie at the airport with a set of bagpipes. Pause for a photo of my futile attempt to play the thing, another snap of me wearing a kilt, followed by a highly-publicised trip round the city, along the banks of Loch Lomond, into the studios of Scottish Television and then back to London.

The pain in my back was steadily increasing. Comedian Michael Bentine had tried heat-transference on me, Katie Boyle had even personally taken me along to her trusted faith-healer, but it was all to no avail. It was time to contact my specialist, Jonathan Beacon. He told me had seen all the publicity and was expecting my call. "We'd better have you back in hospital as soon as possible," he said, so it was next stop Harpenden and a rather gruesome radiculogram. This involves injecting colour-dye into the spinal column to enable experts to have a clear look at soft tissue injuries on a screen. It was like watching a live broadcast from my bed – absolutely fascinating. I could see all the jelly-like gunge that had burst out of my ruptured disc and onto the roots of my nerves at the start of their journey around my body like bits of string. It became clear to Jonathan that I would need an operation to cut the disc away. Daunting, to say the least, but the more immediate problem was the after-effects of the radiculogram. Despite sitting upright as much as possible and drinking pint after pint of water, as advised, I was violently sick for days. I felt terrible, constantly nauseous, so much so that I had to cancel working with

Princess Diana for the first time. That was bitterly disappointing because I had really been looking forward to it. She was a great fan of TVam and had specifically asked for me to present some awards alongside her. A car came to take me from home in Berkhamsted to the Savoy Hotel, but Jill and I had to send it away as I could not even stand up without being sick. On top of all that, I received a letter that morning to say I had not been chosen to host a new game show for which I had been auditioning over recent weeks. In the end, they called it Catchphrase and the chosen presenter was comedian Roy Walker. Undoubtedly the better choice, but that was hardly the best week of my television career!

Bruce Gyngell, who had come in as managing-director over a year earlier, asked me to postpone my operation until January so I would be there to present programmes over the important Christmas period. I was booked in for January 3rd and pain-killers would keep me sane in the meantime. Even so, it hurt like hell, but an amazing thing happened when Jill and I went out for a boozy night with friends in Hemel Hempstead. I had a skinful and, as we left the Jade Lotus Chinese restaurant, I told Jill the pain had gone for the first time in weeks. "You're just p****d," she said. I then attempted the usual agonising procedure of getting into a car and, hey presto, it did not hurt! The problem had cured itself and the shock-absorber gel from the disc had melted away like snow, as my specialist had said it sometimes did. It was a fantastic relief. I was soon leading a normal life again without constant pain and even able to get back onto the squash court. The whole episode had clouded my life for months since I caused the injury by pushing too hard when I was trying to assemble a stubborn wardrobe. A couple of years later, I ruptured another disc, this time when I was lifting little Chris into a pushchair by the Grand Union Canal. It is all about angles! I had loads of physiotherapy, but again an operation was on the cards, until the problem cleared itself. They say if you can be lucky with your bad luck, then you are truly fortunate!

I must make a special mention of my colleagues in the props department at TVam during this time – John, Billy and Russell. I had not been able to sit comfortably on the sofa while my back was so painful, so they did their very best to make things easier for me. They got hold of a large board for me to sit on and covered it with the same orange-coloured material as the sofa's, so nobody would have known. Except that it made me tower above everyone else because they would sink into the plush cushions! Elsewhere, I had to make the best of a difficult situation. When Anne arrived for work at 4 am, she would find me perusing my research details lying on my back. It obviously became a talking point on the programme, to the extent that Princess Diana asked for an update on my condition when she first met Anne!

At the end of all the hilarity and drama of Pamela Stephenson's visit in November 1985, beautiful Pamela herself was very apologetic, especially as she had no idea about my back problem. She was asked by the press if she was ashamed. "Certainly not," she replied. "Children love seeing people drop their trousers. It's very funny and I sure helped to brighten up Nick's image." Pamela later rang me up to invite me to a party she and husband Billy Connolly were holding, but I was unable to make it. Billy, incidentally, is another comedy guest who is a joy to interview and he has never made a grab for my trousers. The only other physical attacks I have suffered on television both involved Rod Hull and Emu. He once attacked John Stapleton and me at TVam and then, many years later, he laid into me when I was presenting a regional light entertainment show for Westcountry TV in Plymouth. The assault was so quick and such a surprise on the second occasion that he sent me flying off a small stage still in my chair and Rod caught me himself with his free hand!

One final word about Pamela Stephenson. About a year after the trousers fracas, she guested again on the programme, but this time I had already moved on to ITV Sport. On this occasion, she persuaded showbiz editor Jason Pollock to provide her with some raw eggs some of which she promptly broke over presenter Geoff Meade's head. The rest she threw over Wincey's weather board. No-one was amused. The studio staff refused to clean up the mess and outside contractors had to be called in to do the job at cost of hundreds of pounds. There was talk of banning Pamela from the studios, but I am not sure whether that ever actually happened.

Anne and I made a trip to Los Angeles in the summer of '85 that included a visit to the home of the great Bob Hope. We were marking thirty years of Disneyland by presenting three programmes live from that mystical place of make-believe with the magic castle as our backdrop. It was a quite wonderful experience and slightly strange as we were broadcasting late at night for a breakfast audience back home. Among our live guests, we chatted to the actor Michael Praed, the actress Margot Kidder, the best-selling novelist Jackie Collins and Anne's heart-throb, Patrick Duffy, who played Bobby Ewing in Dallas. I will never forget Anne's glee before she had seen Patrick that evening, when she was interviewing members of the crowd standing round our makeshift studio. Suddenly, one of the onlookers grabbed her and gave her a passionate kiss, smack on the lips. Who was it? Patrick, of course.

We also recorded a number of interviews with stars at their homes in Beverley Hills or at the Hollywood studios. We spoke to Ned Beatty, Bette Midler, Richard Dreyfus and someone whom I had admired (well, allright then, lusted after) since I was a teenager, Jane Fonda. When I recalled all the posters that had draped my bedroom walls, it was almost surreal to be sitting alongside her on a sofa and gazing into her eyes. How my university mates would have envied me! There's a poignant memory too. We spent some hours at the lovely Malibu home of Pierce Brosnan and his gorgeous wife Cassandra Harris. This was years before he became James Bond. At the time, he was well known for Remington Steele. We had a fabulous chat, lots of laughs, and an exhilarating walk along the beach by their home. Tragically, Cassandra, who herself had once starred in a Bond film, For Your Eyes Only, succumbed to ovarian cancer six years after that lovely day we spent with her in the California sunshine.

We had a team coach to get us around on that trip to Los Angeles, which carried our camera crew and production staff, plus, of course, Anne and me. The party included our Showbusiness Editor, Jason Pollock, and his research assistant, Trish Williamson, who went to present the weather at TVam and later at ITN. Our driver had the devil of a job negotiating some of the narrow lanes around Beverley Hills. More than once, Jason had to get out, knock on doors and ask people if they would mind moving their cars so that we could continue our journey. That journey took us to the splendid home of one of the world's most renowned comics, Bob Hope. In his early eighties, he was a revered elder statesman of showbiz. Little did we know at the time that he would live to be a hundred. I found it particularly exciting to meet him because, not only was I a fan, but my father was a huge admirer of Bob and his sidekick, Bing Crosby. I knew how much he would have loved to have been there with me, so it was a great thrill to get Bob to sign a copy of his autobiography for him. "To Bertie, Enjoy, Best Wishes, Bob Hope."

He was an extremely friendly host. We were joined by his wife, Dolores, and we enjoyed drinks on the patio looking out onto the small golf course in his back garden. We filmed him playing a few shots, we wandered around chatting and then conducted the interview itself. We had a slight wobble when Anne asked Bob how he would like to be remembered, which he clearly took to be a question for an obituary. He visibly stiffened, but we moved on soon enough and we left with a charming and amusing piece for our show that night from Disneyland.

It is not always the easiest task to interview comedians. It is crucial not to upset their timing if they are telling an anecdote and it is also unrealistic to expect them to go through a whole routine of gags. Some can be quite dour when they are not actually performing, while others are just a laugh a minute with hardly a serious word at all. Such a one is Frank Carson. The whole crew are in fits by the time he has finished, on air or off. I remember he greeted Anne one time like this; "Anne, great to see you. I watched you the other day on Miss World and I thought you were robbed. Still, you're certain to win next week… Horse of the Year!"

One man you will rarely see on a chat-show is my close friend Jasper Carrott. I feel privileged to have interviewed him a number of times live, but, in general, he is concerned that an interviewer can disrupt his flow at just the wrong time and ruin the moment. Jasper is a man of astonishing versatility. He is a musician, as well as a comic, and he has performed in sitcoms, opera, West End stage shows and, of course, his sensational one–man shows. More on him later.

Frankie Howerd became a regular contributor during the first year of TVam with an off-beat look at the week's news. He refused to be interviewed by a woman for some reason, so it was always up to me and the format had to be meticulously scripted, with him knowing exactly what I was going to ask next. It was a pleasure to work with him, even if I felt I was clamped in a straight-jacket, but I am not sure he enjoyed it too much. He became mighty nervous before joining us on the sofa and caffeine was not the only substance in his pre-show coffee. He reeked of brandy.

Bob Monkhouse was a joy to interview - the master as far as many comics are concerned and I can well understand why - and I also cherish the memories of mayhem with Billy Connolly, Brian Conley, Frank Skinner, Lenny Henry and Michael Barrymore, irrespective of what occurred in his life in later, sadder times. I must also mention the evergreen Des O'Connor, who has interviewed so many people himself, he knows just what is required when he is facing the questions. Highly amusing, and fascinating too after a desperately difficult childhood.

May 8th is a date engraved in history, marking the allies' victory in Europe in 1945. Forty years on, we planned a huge celebration at Egg Cup Towers in Camden as our futuristic building was known, because of its large egg cups stationed along the roof. The whole programme was turned over to reminiscences and we even had a host of wartime veterans, sitting at tables outside in the forecourt to add atmosphere to this historic anniversary celebration. Among our distinguished guests that day was one Spike Milligan, one of the funniest and most eccentric men that ever lived. He, of course, had seen service in the Second World War and he joined us to deliver a brief resume of his memories of VE Day. Something went horribly wrong with our timings and, when I say his appearance was brief, I mean it. Spike himself was not amused and later that day sent us one of the funniest letters I have ever read.

"Dear All, You remember me. I am the one who went into the Guinness Book of Records, on the 8th May, 1985, for the world's shortest appearance on TVam. I did phone to find out whether I had committed a mortal sin of some kind, but I could not get anybody. Among one of the stories was Jason Pollock was having lunch with the Duke of Edinburgh. (Until that remark I thought I was the funny one).

"I really am absolutely baffled. I was on so briefly, why didn't you just ask me to phone in the item? My manager briefed me, via a briefing from Jason Pollock, and she said, "Spike, they want you to say what you were doing on VE Day," and, in my own humorous way, I told the interviewer. I can't remember his name, because he is one of the unending flow of different people that appear on TVam with the rapidity of legionnaires' disease.

"When I arrived, I saw this dying crowd of tea party people being frozen to death in the forecourt of your bastion, and a chap took me circuitous route, and when I asked him why, he said, "so they don't see you and you don't see them". I said to him, "I've already seen them and I am deeply moved," as I thought they were a set for the last camp for Scott of the Antarctic.

"Anyhow, the circuitous route ended up with somebody offering me a cup of coffee, which looked as though it had been drunk seven times before. They could not get me in the coffee room because it was crowded out, and then somebody said to me "you have got to go out with them", them being the dying survivors of the bombing of London in World War Two and I said," For God's sake, I was never told this, I am only wearing a thin shirt and I have just got out of a hot bath, and it's very cold out there." In the light of this, I had no intention of 'going out there.'

"Then a nice plump Jewish girl said, "Would you like a cup of coffee," then an ordinary Caucasian girl said, "Would you like a cup of coffee", then another man came and did not ask me to have a cup of coffee, and I asked him what had gone wrong with the system, and he said, "I have come to bung a microphone on you." He then searched me with the despair of a tailor who had never heard of pockets. Finally, I said, "There's a pocket here, my son", and so not to overtax his brain, I actually opened it for him so he could drop the thing in. Then suddenly I was rushed into the studio which was in one of the commercial breaks, and I made all your men on the machines have a laugh, telling them the people in the street outside would never last the day out. In fact, a mortician was bringing the hearse that very moment to take some of them home early, in time to say farewell to their relatives. They then announced to the camera, "Welcome back, and guess who's here, it's Spike Milligan." "Tell me, Spike, what were you doing on VE Day? "

"I told them. It lasted 1 minute 40 seconds. I was then marched out of the room in the same manner that Lord Haw-Haw was marched to his death in the Tower in 1946. People turned their backs as I passed them, and then somebody offered me another cup of coffee, then I was shown into a very large room, which I believe is an exact replica of the Gas Chamber at Dachau; there I stood lonely, until ex-Paratrooper Hans Teske, who had actually shot at me in North Africa in 1943, came over and said, "Zieg Heil, Spike," whereupon the Jewish girl said, "Your car is waiting for you," then the confusion, having taken me a mile out of my way to avoid the street party people, I was then marched directly through the middle of them.

"One of them kissed my hand and said, "God bless you sir, and your wife the Queen," and then said," Anytime you're Lambeth way, any evening, any day, you'll find us all freezing to death outside TVam."

"I was picked up by a bearded man called Dan, who said, "Where are you going", and I said wittily, "I am going in your car" and I made yet another enemy.

"Now the Guinness Book of Records comes into play again. I was back to bed asleep before your programme ended. It is now midday and I am still watching the screen in the hope that I might appear.

"Never mind, there will be another VE Day in 40 years time. Can you book me for it now? I will wear a woolly so I can sit outside and eat those appalling jam tarts that were being forced down the throats of your street party victims by Goliath.

"I thought a fitting end to the whole thing would be if TVam had been surrounded by Cherokee Indians on horseback and set on fire with flaming arrows and John Wayne, being de-frozen out of his embalming tube, could say, "Gord darn it."

"Basically, I was so hurried in and hurried out that I feel something had gone wrong.

"Love, light and sleeplessness, Spike."

Wow, some letter, eh? I have to agree with him that it was somewhat chaotic that day and I am appalled that we only had such a short time with him. It is not the only case of what should be a classic interview cut short by a producer's strict adherence to rigid timings. We feel short-changed as presenters, not to say embarrassed, having to cut off guests who have made a special effort and even changed their schedules to be with us. I know of one or two over the years who have been furious afterwards and I remember Rolf Harris saying to me after one very brief chat on Good Morning with Anne and Nick, "I really wonder why I bothered. An utter waste of my time." Pace is very important on magazine programmes, most shows really, but you still have to give people the time they deserve and make cuts elsewhere with a recorded item that can be used at another time. If any great fans of Spike Milligan had tuned in that day to see him, I think they would have been outraged to see only one hundred seconds of him in a three and a half hour show.

Sadly, Spike is no longer with us, but the memory of that day and his letter afterwards still make me laugh now, as did that famous suggestion of his for his epitaph, "I told you I was ill!"

Chapter Eight

BATHTIME WITH ELTON

A great bonus of this job is getting the chance to meet childhood heroes. This has happened to me countless times during my days with TVam, ITV Sport, Good Morning with Anne and Nick and still now with BBC Midlands Today. The names that adorned the celebrity landscape when I was growing up suddenly became regular guests on the programmes I was presenting. I have already mentioned a number, such as Eric Morecambe, but I am particularly thinking of the pop stars who dominated the charts from the late fifties into the sixties. Cliff Richard, Russ Conway, Marty Wilde, Tommy Steele, Adam Faith, the Beatles, Rolling Stones, Animals, Gerry and the Pacemakers, the Searchers, Manfred Mann, Billy J.Kramer, Brian Poole and the Tremeloes, Cilla Black, Dusty Springfield, Lulu and many, many more. I had dealings with all of them and it was special, without exception, almost every time.

My first contact with a Beatle occurred during an hilarious morning with Ringo Starr. He joined us on the breakfast sofa for the launch of Thomas the Tank Engine on television, which he narrated. He was on spectacular form and took great pleasure in disrupting the cookery spot, with a glass of red wine in his hand at 8.30 am! It was also at TVam that Paul McCartney phoned in after he had been offended by a remark on the show from Dionne Warwick. She was claiming that, when the Beatles were in the United States, they had hijacked her hit, Anyone Who Had a Heart, for their friend back home on Merseyside, Cilla Black. Quite a surprise when your producer tells you via the earpiece that McCartney's waiting to talk to you on the blower! Funnily enough, Paul also phoned some ten years later during Good Morning with Anne and Nick on the day we played one of his new singles. I admitted on air I had missed it because of a call of nature! He gave me a mild rollocking, then wrote me a letter and enclosed a copy of the CD. "You'll have to learn to control yourself, man!" he said.

We turned a whole programme over to Adam Faith in April 1985 to mark his twenty-five years in show business. It lasted two hours and came live from the Savoy Hotel. Adam spent a large part of his life either there or at his other famous haunt, the prestigious store, Fortnum and Mason. I was delighted to get to know Adam better because I had bought a number of his early hit records, such as What Do You Want, Poor Me, Someone Else's Baby and When Johnny Comes Marching Home. He had a real jack-the-lad character about him which made him so irresistible to women, I suppose, and made him perfect for the television series, Budgie, and later the touring production of Alfie. I remember in the late fifties when the joy of pop music was starting to sweep inexorably through young minds, I had quite a row with my mother. As a classically trained pianist and music teacher, she really did not approve and was appalled when I dominated conversation at a smart tea party with my thoughts on the charts. I was only about twelve at the time. Still, she and my father changed as the years rolled on, so much so they went of their own accord to a Shadows concert in Great Yarmouth during a touring holiday of East Anglia in the mid-sixties! They came to love the Beatles too, although my father did tell me in 1963 they would be forgotten by next Christmas!

So it was that TVam planned this special about Adam. I met him for lunch with our showbiz researcher Trish Williamson, who had, by coincidence, recently been employed by Adam. By the time of the programme itself, we had a good relationship and the guests we had invited meant it looked a cracker in prospect. How could you go wrong with his old mates sitting round the table, Michael Parkinson, Tim Rice, Elton John and celebrity photographer Terry O'Neill? It was terrific and something I look back on with pride. Michael's son, Nick, was working as a trainee chef at the time at the Savoy, so he joined us for a time and even produced a cake to mark the occasion. Michael had passed fifty the previous week, so he got a cake too. What he could have done without, though, was Elton's little faux-pas. In the early hours, Elton decided to phone from his hotel room in the Savoy his then wife, Renata, in America. He ran a bath first and promptly forgot about it. At roughly 3am, Michael and Mary Parkinson were awoken by the drip-drip of water from above. They called reception and were told that Elton was in the room directly over theirs and his bath had drastically overflowed. In fact, the water invaded three floors and the damage cost around £60,000 to repair. So that gave us a bit to talk about on the show, but my abiding memory is of the final moments, when Elton and Adam sang a duet of 'What Do You Want'. Then the rest of the guests joined us for what became a choral version, before Elton sang us out solo with Too Young, a number from his Ice on Fire album. How privileged I felt to be standing there as one of the world's most illustrious figures gave us an impromptu, live performance. Just Elton and the piano. Wonderful!

Adam wrote me a lovely letter afterwards, which I treasure. 'Dear Nick, Just a few lines to thank you for putting up with us all. Hope we were not too unruly. I thought you coped beautifully. Good luck for the future and again thank you for helping to make Thursday a smashing breakfast. Yours, Adam.'

I saw Adam occasionally in the following years, including a visit backstage when he came to Birmingham on tour with Alfie. I was so shocked and saddened in March, 2003, when he died of a heart attack in the Potteries at the comparatively young age of 62. Ironically, his final television interview was for the programme I now present, BBC Midlands Today.

Gerry Marsden of Pacemakers fame was at the forefront of the Mersey music boom in the early sixties and he was a football fan to boot, so it seemed natural to him to try and raise money to help victims of the sickening fire disaster at Bradford City Football Club in May 1985. The match against Lincoln City in front of an 11,000 crowd was meant to be a celebration for Bradford after they had clinched the championship of the old Third Division. It turned to utter tragedy when fire broke out just before half time and swept through a stand at their Valley Parade ground. Fifty six supporters died and 265 were injured. It roared through the largely wooden stand in a matter of minutes. It is thought to have been caused by the accidental dropping of a match or cigarette end into a polystyrene cup and the flames were soon fuelled by rubbish underneath the stand. Not surprisingly, it went down as the worst fire disaster in the history of British football.

Gerry Marsden gathered together a load of his pop music pals and brought out a special version of his iconic football anthem, "You'll Never Walk Alone". Many of the country's best known musicians took part in the recording of the single and added their own personal messages on the B side. The cash raised went towards the Bradford Disaster Fund, which altogether brought in £3.5 million for the victims and their families. Gerry was due to appear on TVam on May 30th to promote the song and tell us why he felt moved to become involved.

By a bizarre irony, another dreadful football tragedy happened the night before and this time it was even closer to home for Gerry. Crowd trouble before Liverpool's European Cup Final against Juventus at the Heysel Stadium in Brussels led to a wall collapsing and the eventual death of 39 supporters, most of them from Italy. Four hundred others were injured. The blame fell on the Liverpool fans for charging towards their rivals under provocation, but poor organisation at the stadium resulted in both sets of fans being stationed in the same area, separated only by a flimsy fence. So, remarkably, on the morning after the appalling night before, we had one of the best-known and best-loved Liverpudlians in the world with us on the sofa. And he was there originally to talk about a different footballing tragedy. From a hard-nosed journalistic point of view, it was excellent to have such a high-profile and prestigious spokesman for Merseyside, but how desperately difficult it must have been for Gerry. We were also joined by Jimmy Greaves and the writer Ian Woolridge on a sad day for our national sport. In the end, all English clubs were banned from Europe for five years, with Liverpool serving a further two years after that. The result seems totally irrelevant, but Liverpool lost 1-0. Staggering really that they actually played a football match after the carnage beforehand.

Desperately sad as it was that morning with Gerry Marsden, Anne and I usually enjoyed far happier mornings chatting to pop stars. I have already talked about our time with the Bee Gees, but they had no idea of the difficulty we had when we were invited to the premiere of their musical, Staying Alive. Anne, Wincey and I had not exactly mastered the art of style. In fact, I still have a long way to go in this department. Anyway, on this particular night in September 1983, we travelled together to Leicester Square in London by taxi. Mistake. When we arrived, there was no way in which we could get near enough in the cab because of the hordes of fans there hoping for a glimpse of the film's stars, John Travolta and Finola Hughes, or any other celebrities strutting across the red carpet. We had to disembark, battle our way through the serried ranks and then clamber over the metal barriers. Difficult enough for me, near impossible for Anne and Wincey in their smart frocks. So undignified! All the time people were asking for our autographs and wondering how we came to be where we came to be! As we dusted ourselves down and regained our composure, we saw a smart limo pull up on the right side of the barriers and out stepped our esteemed colleague David Frost, unruffled, no hassle, dignity intact. This was how it was meant to be. We also watched David cruise away afterwards, as we vainly sought a taxi to take us home. No chance, so we walked and walked and walked, pursued by scores of curious TVam fans, wondering why we had not taken a limo like just about everyone else at the premiere! In the end, we hastened down the steps of the underground and made our way by tube.

I look back fondly on a visit in that first year from the Animals pop group. I had bought nearly all their tracks in the sixties including House of the Rising Sun, Please Don't Let Me Be Misunderstood and We Gotta Get Outa This Place, so it was terrific to spend time with them, especially as all five came. That was quite an achievement, as they were not getting on too well with each other at the time. Eric Burdon, I think, has one of the most powerful voices in pop history. Strong, earthy and evocative. Dusty Springfield I missed at TVam because I was on a day off, but at least she posed in the TVam foyer for a photograph next to a picture of me! Not seeing her then was quite a blow because I had just loved her during my schooldays.

Looking across the decades of pop, we interviewed Motown legends such as Martha Reeves of Vandellas fame, Mike Rutherford,

Tony Banks and Phil Collins, of Genesis, Rick Wakeman, Lonnie Donegan, Acker Bilk, Bill Wyman, Simon Le Bon, Suzi Quatro, Andy Fairweather-Low, Gloria Gaynor, Status Quo and many, many more just in the first few months as the programme began to catch fire.

Anne and I were naturally well researched on our sixties idols, because we had grown up with them, but we found it a lot harder to get to grips with the emerging artists who were hitting the charts for the first time. I remember one exasperated young researcher having to promise us that this new duo called Wham! really were going places and that George Michael would be a huge star.

We needed no telling about David Essex. What a remarkable guy he is! So laid-back, natural and friendly, with a timeless appeal that seems to cross the generations. I have been to many of his concerts, where the age range of his audience shows just how his music and charisma gets through to all ages. He always gives up time to meet up with his fans afterwards, either in a special hospitality area behind the scenes or outside the stage door. We have met up on countless occasions and I am always struck by his willingness to give his time to people. In fact, sometimes he gives people a very good time indeed. In the mid-eighties, when he was promoting Mutiny, the musical he had written about the mutiny on the Bounty, he held a party on board a boat on the Thames. What a great day that was, as we cruised up and down the river in the sunshine. David played host, of course, alongside the actor Frank Finlay who was playing the part of Captain Bligh in the musical. David was Fletcher Christian in a show that suffered a bit of a panning from the critics, but proved very popular with the public. Wincey came with me on the cruise and the wine flowed liberally. I seem to remember she became very tired very quickly. I spent hours on deck soaking up the fresh air and chatting to the singer Marti Webb. Marti is a close friend of David's and, like him, she is great company, with a terrific sense of humour. She had already been a guest on our programme and we have met up a number of times socially over the years. There is no need to talk much either....she never stops!

Tahiti, the best-known song from the musical, made the top ten long before the show itself actually reached the stage. It really caught my imagination and, even now, it instantly takes me back to those early, often troubled, days at TVam. Things were far from easy domestically because, for the first two and a half years of breakfast television, home was still in Birmingham. Our two young children were settled in their school, we had a lovely home and Jill had a good job. Coupled with that was the uncertainty over the company's future, so we had little inclination to move south and put all our eggs in one basket. However, it made life very tough for Jill. I was away five days a week in my tiny flat in north London and she had to cope with her nursing work and two demanding little boys. When I came home at the weekends, all I really wanted to do was sleep, which was hardly fair on anyone. The children wanted to play with Dad and Jill wanted a breather. Andrew and Tim saw more of me on the box than in real life. Amid the welter of publicity about breakfast television at the time, they began to see me as others did, rather than their father. One time, I got back from London and Tim shouted out, "Nick Owen's here!" Jill replied, "Well, get him to sign the visitors' book."

After one domestic crisis too many in my absence, we decided the time had come to move, so we headed for my spiritual home of Berkhamsted in the summer of 1985. We sold our spacious, four bedroomed house with big garden in Birmingham for about sixty grand and bought a box with a tiny, fiercely sloping patch of grass for the best part of a hundred. Reality check! For me, it was wonderful to be back in the town where I had grown up, particularly as I had missed it so much when I was at boarding school and university. By chance, we had to move back to the Midlands in the nineties for Good Morning with Anne and Nick and we are very happy here, but I will always be a Hertfordshire boy deep down, with a longing for the rolling green of the Chiltern Hills. Andy and Tim feel that way too, having spent some important early years of their lives there, and they share my passion for nearby Luton Town Football Club. Jill, on the other hand, still has friends in Berkhamsted and she is well settled in Birmingham, but she is more naturally drawn to Chester, where she grew up.

So those early days at TVam were often full of fun, laughter and excitement, but there was always the lurking fear that investors might pull the plug. When the maximum viewers in any one quarter of an hour spell fell as low as 200,000, advertising rates dropped to £700 a minute. Two years later, when at least two million a day were watching, advertisers were paying up to £15,000 a minute. In the intervening times, board meetings came and went, with the workforce hanging on every announcement. Would we all have jobs tomorrow? All 350 staff took a pay cut at one stage, while Anne and I had an anxious couple of months in '83, banging on the door of accounts asking for our next cheque. We were on air one day when we were told through our ear-pieces that the power could go off any time and the whole building and programme would be plunged into darkness. Apparently, the company had failed to pay the electricity bill. Luckily, Greg arrived in the nick of time and paid out of his own account.

Following the announcement of a multi-million pound refinancing package to save the company in November 1983, the famed Australian tycoon Kerry Packer took a ten per cent stake in the company. Within six months, he put Bruce Gyngell in as managing director to supervise swingeing cuts in our operating costs. Bruce, a legend down-under, where he had been the first face on Australian television, was looking to save as much as £3million a year. Greg did not get on too well with him or his plans and he resigned within weeks. It was not long before editor Clive Jones left too…in protest at Bruce's decision to withdraw from our planned comprehensive coverage of the Olympic Games in Los Angeles. I was going to be presenting it, so I was disappointed too. Little did I know then that I would be anchoring the next games, four years later in Seoul, as ITV Sport's main presenter. Bruce wanted to cut staff numbers and was accused at a union meeting of merely being a bean counter. "You can do it in Alice Springs, but not here at Camden Lock," he was told. Bruce said to John Stapleton he wanted to reduce his presenting days and get him on the road more. That was not in John's contract, so he too decided on a parting of the ways. John's wife, Lynn Faulds Wood, soon followed. She had been in the building from the hard hat days, but Bruce told her he felt her type of consumer journalism was not appropriate on breakfast television. I was extremely sad to see them all go.

Greg had been an inspirational leader. I accept that he took us downmarket, but I prefer to look at it in a different way. He made us more watchable to more people. He made us smile and he gave the audience what they clearly wanted at that time of day. He created the structure that became the blueprint throughout the life of TVam and GMTV afterwards. The alternative was to go bust. It is not as if we ignored the serious news stories of the day, but we were strapped for resources, so there were times when we had no chance of matching the BBC for comprehensive coverage of a major event. One master-stroke on that score was Greg's idea to bring veteran ITN newscaster Gordon Honeycombe on board. Greg reckoned that, even if the picture coverage and detail was sometimes a little sparse, Gordon's heavyweight presence at the newsdesk would always add credibility. I later worked for Greg when he was chairman of the ITV Sports Committee and, after that, when he became Director General of the BBC. Every time, he has been great company, full of ideas, relentlessly energetic and a genuine friend of the shop floor. Like everyone else at the BBC, I was shattered when he felt forced to resign in the wake of severe criticism of the corporation in the Hutton report. Jill and I, with our two youngest children, Chris and Jenny, bumped into Greg, John and their respective families completely by chance in Portugal in the summer of 2002. We went shark fishing together the next day. Amazingly, Greg dived in when we were six miles offshore in an ocean that was meant to be full of sharks. Crazy! Hardly man-eaters, I know, but you would never have got John or me doing that. What is more, we nearly dislocated our shoulders trying to haul him back on board. For the record, we never saw a single dorsal. We were not to know then what turbulent waters Greg would be facing in the coming years at the BBC.

A special word for John, deservedly named Presenter of the Year for 2004 by the Royal Television Society. We got on really well at TVam and still keep in touch. We both love our football....he follows Manchester City and Oldham Athletic, but I understand he is having treatment. We both have the same sense of humour and still laugh about the day he was due to handle a heavy interview during a strike by shipbuilders. Anne and I had noticed in the newspaper that an official of the Shipbuilders Association was a certain Mr. Noah, which kind of amused us. We bantered about it before handing over to John, who then introduced the shipbuilding union leader as Mr. Alex Ferry! As Anne and I tried to contain ourselves, he proceeded to ask Mr. Ferry if he felt his members had been sold down the river! I have tremendous regard for John and, indeed, for Lynn. Thank goodness she was able to fight so bravely and successfully against bowel cancer in the early nineties. I am only sorry that they and many others who went through hoops of fire in the tortuous first year were unable to toast the huge success that TVam later enjoyed.

Chapter Nine

MAGGIE AND THE RAT

Presenting a magazine programme on radio or television gives you tremendous variety and the inevitable challenge of moving tastefully through the topics of the day, from happy to sad, hilarious to serious. I have interviewed six British Prime Ministers over the years, in or out of office, but they are quite likely to have shared the sofa with a sex-god, boy band or merciless comic storing up material for the future. Those Prime Ministers, incidentally, are Harold Wilson, Jim Callaghan, Edward Heath, Margaret Thatcher, John Major and Tony Blair. Edward Heath, with his stentorian voice, was always hugely entertaining at TVam. He was becoming an elder statesman by then and delighted in taking an acerbic look at political events of the time. He had a ready wit and was always quick to take the mickey out of a wide-eyed, sometimes naive, interviewer! My abiding memory of Mrs. Thatcher was a chance meeting with her at a ceremony to celebrate children who had achieved success against the odds. I was chatting to a little boy who had won an award, when Mrs. T came up to join us. A look of utter bewilderment swept across her face, as he told her with barely concealed admiration. "This is Roland Rat's dad!" She probably had no idea who Roland was, because she once told us, "I never watch your programme, but I gather I am on it rather a lot!"

I have had more to do with John Major than any other Prime Minister. Besides interviewing him, I have inevitably bumped into him on numerous occasions at cricketing events and one deserves special mention. On the retirement of Warwickshire and England fast bowler Gladstone Small, a number of Gladstone's friends, led by fellow fast bowler and good egg Tim Munton, decided to stage a surprise farewell dinner for him at the Metropole Hotel near the NEC, just outside Birmingham. I was asked to act as Master of Ceremonies for an extremely popular and charismatic figure and it turned into a truly wonderful and emotional evening. For a start, Gladstone thought he was about to have dinner merely with a couple of friends and his wife Lois. They entered the huge ballroom in semi-darkness, only for the lights to come up and reveal hundreds of cheering friends and admirers. His face was a picture. We screened video messages from playing colleagues across the world plus generous tributes from fellow internationals at the dinner itself. His children turned up, which was an emotional moment in itself, but accompanying them were his Mum and Dad and brother, who had flown in from Barbados. He had not seen them for more than two years. They had been staying with his sister for a few days, praying that Gladstone would not find out. Lois's parents also came in from Australia along with her sister... again, they had not seen each other for a couple of years. Then, to cap it all, the former Prime Minister. He was booked to attend another dinner in the same hotel, Tim and co. found out about it, waylaid him in the foyer and he was delighted to become involved. In fact, he strode in at about 9.15 even before he had done his job elsewhere, and, along with a couple of well-received cricketing anecdotes, delivered his own kind words about Gladstone. Thunderous applause and a fitting climax to a superb evening.

Talking of politicians, it is not often I feel sorry for them, but I did have a little sympathy for an MP in February 1985, round about the end of the fierce and bitter miners' strike. We had invited Tory MP Edwina Currie and Labour member for the Rhondda, Alan Rogers, to the studio, with no particular brief about the subject matter, but both held mining constituencies. Edwina was first in and sitting with us on the sofa, when our floor manager told us Mr. Rogers had arrived. Edwina looked up and told us, "That's not Alan Rogers, it's Alan Roberts, Member for Bootle. His constituency has no connection with the mining industry." It seemed the message for Alan Rogers had found its way into the next door pigeon-hole, so the wrong man turned up. Alan Roberts bravely agreed to join us, though, and we all had a laugh about it before the real business got under way. Edwina was extremely gracious to her Labour opponent off air, joking away, but, once the cameras started rolling, the gloves came flying off and she slaughtered him. She had considerable specialist knowledge, of course, from her mining patch of South Derbyshire. Her classic killer thrust went something like this, "But how can YOU know anything about it…you don't even have any pits in your constituency!" All is fair in love and war, I suppose, but it did seem a bit harsh on a bloke who was doing us a last-minute favour. We were all laughing our socks off under the surface!

Through the Keyhole first emerged on British television in the very first week of TVam and proved a notable success amongst all the disappointment. It was presented by the then unknown figure of Loyd Grossman, who took us around celebrity houses in a short film. That was followed by a live studio interview with the 'victim.' There was no hint of mystery about it then. That came later when Through the Keyhole was successfully converted into a half hour panel game of 'guess whose house it is.' Loyd was extremely amusing, but rather harsh and a number of celebrities left the building smarting at his barbs about their treasured homes. After one notorious slating, the actress Patricia Hayes was so upset that her management agency swore they would never send another of their clients our way again and they stood by their word for some considerable time. Poor Pat left the building in tears and we had to tell Loyd to pull back from then on. I also recall a world champion boxer arriving at the studio and asking us not to run our film about his home. He was with his girlfriend and apparently she did not know he was married and had a separate home!

Gyles Brandreth became a valued friend and colleague in those early days of breakfast television, but Anne and I were somewhat sceptical before his first appearance. We had no idea who he was, although he had already built up a bit of a reputation as a raconteur, wit, Monopoly champion, holder of any off-the-wall world record that might be available, writer of children's books and all-round eccentric. Well, he was absolutely electrifying on the sofa and soon became a regular fixture on the programme. His pretext for joining us each week was to talk about new video releases, but he contributed so much more than that. He became famous for his ever more audacious woolly jumpers, appeared on a host of quiz programmes, became an even more prolific author, wrote the world's shortest poem, won the world Scrabble title and ended up in Parliament for five years as a Conservative MP. The last time I saw him, Anne and I were guests on his This is Your Life programme, which was hilarious, largely due to his phenomenal sense of humour.

Similarly to Gyles, Paul Gambaccini reviewed new films for us on a regular basis and he, too, brought far more than that to the table. What struck us all at the studio was his astonishing ability to deliver a two minute verdict on a film, directly to camera, which was word perfect, without a hint of hesitation, and with no autocue or notes of any kind. Paul was already a well-known disc jockey and music journalist in this country, having made his home here after leaving the United States, and he was strikingly bright. He gained a History degree in America and then took Philosophy, Politics and Economics at Oxford. Not many people on breakfast television at the time had two degrees! To this day, he is often the first expert that news organisations call upon if they need some independent analysis of a story from the world of music. Paul recently celebrated thirty years in broadcasting and I felt honoured to be numbered among the illustrious few who attended his celebration at the Ivy restaurant in London. The guests included Dawn French and Lenny Henry, Sir Tim Rice, Sir Cliff Richard, Stephen Fry, Bob Geldoff and Noel Edmonds. Also there was Henry Kelly, who became a good friend in TVam days. He had his own Saturday show there and also stood in when Anne or I took time off. He nearly finished me one day, when we were presenting together. Just before we went on air, he asked me why the controversial tennis star John McEnroe always wore a headband. When the titles had nearly finished rolling and I was within seconds of delivering my opening words, he turned mischievously towards me…"To hide the circumcision scar!" he said.

Besides Anne, my co-presenters included Jayne Irving, Anneka Rice and the actress Nanette Newman. It was the idea of our then programme controller, Mike Hollingsworth, to give Nanette a chance. It was quite a challenge for her, as she obviously found the journalistic/presenting world a little foreign, but any misgivings she may have had were soon dispelled, I am sure, by the warm reception she received from colleagues and viewers. Her engaging personality came effortlessly across. She was harshly self-critical, even in the letter written to me afterwards. "I watched this morning with a cup of coffee in bed. What joy! No mistakes, no fluffs, no starting with 'can I ask you', no teleprompter read too fast, no desperate looks, see? I noticed it all this time". Her husband, the renowned film director Bryan Forbes, was good enough to send me a copy of his book and write a separate letter, thanking me for "being so kind to Nanette." I can assure them both, it was an absolute pleasure! Mind you, I was hardly a veteran of the job myself at the time – I had only been doing it for about a year and a half. Over the intervening years, I have seen Anneka from time to time and remained close friends with Jayne. Jayne was plonked next to Prince Andrew when he came to lunch one time at Egg Cup Towers. She was telling him about some of the methods we were using to bring in new viewers. Amongst other things, we had taken to reading out the Bingo numbers from the Sun newspaper and it was causing uproar with newsagents, who found fewer and fewer people were coming in to buy the paper. It clearly did not cut much ice with the Prince, who simply asked, "But what IS Bingo?"

Wincey was an integral part of TVam's ultimate success. She was always game for a laugh on air and regularly gave me some merciless stick, which was duly returned. I always said Wincey had teeth like the stars. They came out at night. Anne felt like a referee half the time. We were grateful to her for a cunning plan on the day we had a visit from a plethora of Nolan sisters. Anne and I were concerned about remembering which Nolan was which, so Wincey constructed some 'charming' pink cardboard badges with their individual names on and asked the girls to wear them. She pretended they had been sent in by an obsessed fan, John from Leeds, who had begged them to wear them on the programme. I am ashamed to say we even got the Nolans to thank John on camera.

Wincey also had a part to play, unsuccessfully, on the day we had a visit from veteran comedy actor, Norman Wisdom. He could be very funny, but sometimes he needed holding back. Anne was conducting a seriously moving interview with a family hit by tragedy, when

Norman decided to liven things up by staggering on as a daft waiter with a tray of coffee cups. Showbiz editor Jason Pollock desperately tried to restrain him from just behind the cameras, so did Wincey, so did I, but to no avail and Norman strode on towards the action. He wobbled on with coffee cups rattling, but the floor manager pushed him back. Jason grabbed him and pulled him away to the hospitality room. "You really can't do that sort of thing, Norman," Jason told him. "OK," replied Norman with that innocent, cheeky grin of his, "I'll go and read the news." And off he stormed towards the separate news studio, which was the hallowed domain of Gordon Honeycombe. With great difficulty, Jason grabbed his jacket as he headed through the studio door, wrenched him away and led off to breakfast, so ending what could have become a highly embarrassing episode!

The late Victor Kiam joined us for an experiment one morning to decide which was the better shave, wet or dry. He was the shrewd businessman, of course, who famously said in a long running commercial for Remington, "I liked the shaver so much, I bought the company." I have personally always found electric razors a little inadequate, so we decided to have a contest on air. I was asked not to shave for a day in preparation for the grand encounter and we had a barber lined up with a cut-throat to tackle one side of my face. I would dry shave the other. Well, the cut throat certainly did a superb job, though close-up camera work revealed blobs of blood round my chin. The Remington, however, surprised me at how good it was and I said so. At which point, Victor said, "Well, you can have it." I said, "Thank you very much." And that was the end of it, or so I thought, until Greg collared me later and told me I could not accept a gift in that way and I would have to send it back, which I did with a letter of thanks, but no thanks. Pity! On that subject, I also remember a chat on air with Lynn Faulds Wood about the sugar content in Pils lager. I told her I loved the stuff and, even before we were off air, there was a crate of it in reception. I am distinctly unable to remember what happened to it!

We have all had to ask some tricky questions in our time. The Queen's cousin and esteemed photographer, Lord Lichfield, was a guest one time when rumours were rife about his health. He had lost a remarkable amount of weight and looked dangerously gaunt. Did he have AIDS? I checked with him beforehand if I could ask and he was fine about it, but I felt slightly uncomfortable. Probably the first time a member of the Royal family had been asked publicly about something so personal, but happily he was fine and the rumours dispersed. I rather shocked Anne when I asked the luscious Joanna Lumley if she was wearing knickers. That all stemmed from my producer of the day, Chris Riley. He told me down my earpiece that he had heard she often forsook that most delicate of garments....would I dare ask her about it? Well, I did and, correct, she hardly ever did wear knickers! I admit I warned her in a commercial break the question was coming, but Anne was not in on it. Joanna played the part of indignant surprise to perfection and Anne was reeling with embarrassment. Joanna explained that her mother had told her it was healthier to go without them and she was not too keen on the VPL, visible panty line. Just to illustrate, she turned her backside to camera and indicated that perfect form within her tight, white trousers and, of course, no sign of a VPL!

So TVam, with its astonishing range of guests and topics, from the tragic to the trivial, the heavy to the hilarious, was a highly stimulating place to be. Losses turned into profits and commercial breakfast television had established itself on the broadcasting landscape. Up to fifteen million were watching us per week and, as we entered our fourth year, there was a mood of celebration. Gordon Honeycombe said at the time, "Good Morning Britain is a remarkable success story. But I never doubted it would be successful. It was such a bright, happy, energetic team. It reminded me of when I joined ITN, another Cinderella organisation, regarded by everyone as a vulgar little upstart when it began." However, I was bedevilled about my quality of life. Leaving home at ten past three every morning and returning home shattered each afternoon was hardly ideal for family life. I went to bed at eight immediately after Andrew and Tim had had their baths, just as a motor cycle roared up to the house with my briefing notes for the following day. Piles of the stuff, up to three inches thick. I would read for as long as I could before crashing out, while Jill spent many evenings alone downstairs, thinking she was a single mother. We hardly ever went out, except at weekends, and, even then, it was not unknown for me to slump comatose into the Mulligatawny at half past eight! Most days, you would feel reasonably good until mid-morning and then the jet-lag would set in. If I sat down for any time in the afternoon, I would just nod off. Down a couple of pints and I was anybody's. I remember going to a performance of the musical Cats with Wincey in the West End because the composer Andrew Lloyd-Webber was coming on the show the following day. Within minutes, I fell asleep on the front row. I woke up to find myself face-to-face with a grinning dancer who had gleefully spotted I was off in another world. She was right there, close-up, barely three feet away, at the end of a pulsating sequence that just managed to bring me round. That was a matinee. If I went to anything in the evening, usually to see a performer who was due on the show the next day, I would leave at half time. Comedian and friend Jasper Carrott rang me up to say he was coming to London to watch a performance of The Nerd, as he had been offered the main part to follow Rowan Atkinson. Would I go with him? We met in the early evening for a meal, went to the show and, to his mild consternation, I jumped ship, as usual, at the interval. We both liked what we saw, though, and Jasper took over from Rowan for a ten-week tour.

Out of the blue, my old mate from Central, Trevor East, got in touch and suggested we meet for lunch. He was working for the sports department at Thames Television and wondered whether I fancied a return to the fold. It was quite some time before I realised he was offering me the top job as ITV Sport's main presenter. It was a difficult decision to make. TVam was going really well by this stage and I had been offered a new contract, but the nagging question remained; how long could I keep up the life-style demanded by breakfast television? Love it as I did, it was incredibly demanding for someone with a young family, with three hours live television five days a week and a massive amount of preparation required for up to twenty interviews on each programme. Great fun to do, but going back to ITV Sport would mean a chance to rejoin the human race.

In the end, I decided to take the sporting option, although I would be earning less money. I told Bruce Gyngell and I have to say that was not easy. Although he had upset my old colleagues such as Greg Dyke and John Stapleton, I had a lot of time for Bruce. He was certainly different from anyone I had ever known before. He was obsessed with the colour pink and always wore a pink shirt. He had a trampoline in his office to help relieve stress. He wanted to make his television station a caring friend to all. In his own words, "I set out to make TVam eternal summer, so lost, lonely people could turn on and feel warm and bright." He felt so strongly about warm, bright colours that he gave presenters Jayne Irving and Jeni Barnett a fearsome tongue-lashing when their dress sense failed to match up to his sunny requirements. Dark blue, grey, black – total anathema. He went down in Australian history in 1956, when he became the first face on television there. His opening words ran like this, "Good evening, ladies and gentlemen. Welcome to television." He made his mark here too, by continuing the excellent work started by Greg and turning TVam into arguably the most financially successful television station in the world. Rightly or wrongly, Margaret Thatcher became a great admirer for his clinically firm dealings with the unions and apologised to him later for instigating the system that led to the ending of the station's franchise in 1991. She decreed that companies should make a cash bid for the right to broadcast on ITV's Channel 3. Bruce offered just over £14 million a year for the right to carry on as he was, while the company that became GMTV put in an offer of more than £36 million. They won the day, much to everyone's shock, but ironically were never able to afford the amount they bid and had to have it reduced. A rather bitter postscript for the people who lost so much, when TVam finally came to a close. I had long gone by then, but I know what a devastating blow it was to all concerned. Bruce was shattered as he looked disbelievingly at the fax that arrived from the ITC. Bruce went back to Australia before returning here as managing director of Yorkshire Tyne Tees Television in the mid-nineties. Not long afterwards, when I was struggling to make ends meet, he gave me some much needed work and I will always be grateful to him for that. He died of lung cancer in September 2001 at the age of 71, leaving his wife Kathy, a friend and colleague of mine at TVam, and their two young boys, Adam and Jamie.

My final day's broadcast at TVam was highly emotional for me. My editorial colleagues, including Anne and Wincey, planned a programme full of surprises and undoubtedly gave me rousing send-off. Looking back now at a tape from that August Friday in 1986, I see that the missing estate agent Suzy Lamplugh was our top story, D registration car number plates had been introduced for the first time, while the two Steves, Cram and Ovett, were winning gold medals on the track in the Commonwealth Games in Edinburgh, along with Tessa Sanderson in the javelin. We read out addresses without postcodes and Anne and I looked extremely young and fresh-faced. Our sports bulletin that day was presented by Richard Keys, who went on to establish himself as a superbly efficient anchorman for Sky. He wrapped up with a surprise for me and brought on three sporting heroes to say goodbye, former England cricket captain Bob Willis, the current skipper, Mike Gatting, and former Luton Town goalscoring hero, Malcolm Macdonald. The pop singer Kim Wilde, who had become a good friend of the programme, also joined us to say farewell. Wincey then dedicated her last weather forecast of the morning to me saying, "There'll be a deep depression over Camden, believe you me. It's a very sad day." It was all rather overwhelming, but indicative, I think, of a close team who had been through a lot of testing times together. As we approached the end of my last show, I was linking into what turned out to be a non-existent feature with the actor, Frank Finlay. I was halfway through my introduction when I suddenly became aware of a presence behind me - Gyles Brandreth launching into a spoof version of This is Your Life! He described me as the face that had launched a thousand quips, embarrassed me with a collection of childhood photos and embellished it all with a brilliantly amusing script. He called up David Frost, former Luton manager David Pleat, page three models Sam Fox and Linda Lusardi, plus other members of our team, including Jimmy Greaves, Gordon Honeycombe, Wincey and Adrian Brown, who was going to replace me. But what really finished me as a soft old Dad was the arrival of my two little boys, Andrew and Tim. They were meant to be at a sports camp, but when they scampered on and into my arms, it really broke me up for a second or two. They were too shy to open their mouths, "a bit overawed," I said. To which Anne replied, "I think Dad's a bit overawed too!" Anne then delivered the closing link and she lost it too! Afterwards, hundreds of colleagues were standing outside the studio in the magnificent atrium, as I was given a leaving present of a set of golf clubs, plus an antique wheelchair and ear trumpet. Well, I was nearly 39 years old! It was a tearful, yet happy morning to round off a quite unforgettable three and a half years, which had totally changed my life. And there were more changes to come. Besides the news sports job, Jill was pregnant with our third baby, which turned out to be Chris, and a new game show was in the offing, Sporting Triangles.

Watching breakfast television for a few snatched minutes each day had become the norm for millions of people. It seemed that viewers regarded us as friends who spoke the same language. We received some wonderful letters, but one stands out for me, after a little boy called Simon who was suffering from cancer came from the Potteries to visit the studio and meet us all. His mum Carole said, "How can I ever put into words the thanks I have for all the crew at TVam? You have made a little boy's grim year into a dream. After all the nasties of chemotherapy and radiotherapy, his only words are for his special day with you.....Simon's appearance with Roland Rat on the air has really helped him face going back to school. Instead of noticing that he hasn't much hair, all the children are talking about him being Roland Rat superstar. You have saved us from what could have been a very unpleasant situation. We found the visit so interesting, seeing the terrific pressures you are all working under, how you cope with all this so that the viewer is completely unaware of all sorts of difficulties, as you appear relaxed and casual on air. It is nice to think that even under all this strain, you still had time for one little boy. We do appreciate it.

"Please keep up your good work, remembering when things get tough, that there are many people with special problems like Simon, who get so much pleasure from watching your programme. With grateful thanks, Carole."

That wonderful letter moved us all, as you can imagine, and made us realise what a privilege and, indeed, responsibility it was to broadcast our sort of programme to millions of people. I would not have missed it for the world.

Chapter Ten

WORKING WITH NORA

I must have been very naïve, but it never crossed my mind how many people would be upset by my appointment as the main presenter of ITV Sport. What made it worse for Brian Moore, whom I replaced, was the way it was handled. I had worked frequently with him for a number of years and always had the highest regard for him. A genuinely good man, with a real stress on the 'good'. When the move was first mooted, I somehow believed that the change for him from in-vision presenting to concentrate on football commentaries was part of a long-term plan, but quite clearly it was not. The news leaked out to the newspapers before Brian had the remotest inkling that anything was going on. Once Thames Television executives realised it was about to be reported in the papers, they called Brian at home and broke the news. He was stunned and spent the rest of the evening fielding calls from the press. It suited Brian and everyone at Thames to take the line that it was his decision to move out of the studio and focus solely on commentating, but the headlines the next day proclaimed quite clinically that he had been sacked. It was horrible and I felt dreadful. I rang him at home that day from my office at TVam and, first of all, spoke to his wife Betty. She was understandably cool and clearly taken aback to be talking to me. Brian came to the telephone and I apologised for the distress he must have been feeling and for the way things had been handled. It was a conciliatory chat and we continued to get on well in our working lives together over the next six years.

My move back to sport also had repercussions for others and, again, I had not really appreciated the fact in advance. It emerged that my old friend Jim Rosenthal felt his route to the top had been blocked by my arrival. Jim had made his way into television at

London Weekend after a highly successful time as one of the top performers with BBC Radio Sport. It never crossed my mind that he saw himself as Brian's successor on the flagship programme, Midweek Sport Special. He was so involved in other things within ITV Sport that I had not made the connection, but I now know Jim had very strong words with Thames' Head of Sport, Bob Burrows, who was responsible for that particular programme and a number of other network projects. ITV Sport was run as a committee in those days. The individual companies obviously dealt with their own regions' output day-to-day, but came together as a group to make decisions that affected the network's national programming. Martin Tyler, another long-standing friend, was about to be the main commentator at the Mexico World Cup and he now saw his position threatened with Brian returning full-time to the gantry. Within a few years, as any football fan will know, Martin moved on to the freshly-hatched Sky Sports where he has served with such understated expertise and distinction for more than a decade.

Inevitably, Jim was fairly cool in my direction, but it got worse. He had been presenting all ITV Sport's Figure Skating, including European and World Championships overseas. I was told that he had not enjoyed it too much and would be relieved when I took over. Well, he told me some time afterwards that he had never said he disliked ice skating and indeed he was extremely disappointed to be taken off it. Then, to cap it all, I was informed a few months later that the powers-that-be would prefer me to present all ITV's major athletics events. And who was the current incumbent? Yes, of course, Jim. At this stage, with a host of other commitments, besides concern about Jim's position, I had quite enough on my plate so I turned it down – twice. Then it was very firmly put to me that I really must take it on because management wanted me to get my feet under the athletics table in readiness for anchoring the 1988 Olympics to be held in Seoul. So I became the athletics presenter on the platform above the stadium at venues such as Crystal Palace, Birmingham and Gateshead, while Jim took on the reporting and interviewing role trackside. I sensed the discomfort, resentment even, towards me from the production team who believed Jim had been kicked in the guts.

Which he had. It was not always easy from my point of view. I recall one time during a European Cup event at Gateshead, the whole editorial team went out for a meal without telling me. Still, room service was excellent, if a little lonely! Even so, they were good people to work with and I am particularly grateful to commentator Alan Parry and producers Richard Russell and Richard Worth. They were all great mates of Jim's, but professionally totally supportive of us both. I had known them all for some time anyway, so it was not as if a complete stranger had been thrust into the camp, but it must have been tricky for them, to say the least.

While we are talking athletics, I must pick out the World Championships '87 in Rome. As a classicist, it was special for me to spend a couple of weeks in the eternal city, irrespective of some stunning activity in the Olympic Stadium. British athletics were on a high, with a clutch of household names in or close to the medals, including Fatima Whitbread, who won gold in the javelin, Linford Christie, John Regis, Peter Elliott, Jon Ridgeon, Colin Jackson, Derek Redmond and Kris Akabusi. My abiding memory is of the 100 metres final, the build-up and the event itself. The athletics world bristled with rumours that Canadian Ben Johnson's success on the track owed as much to pharmaceutical assistance as his magnificent physique. Carl Lewis, who had won an incredible four golds at the 1984 Olympics and would go on to win five more, made no secret of the fact he despised Johnson and his methods. Their rivalry provided the focal point on that warm August evening as the sun cast a golden glow over the stadium. The place was humming with tension and anticipation in a sell-out crowd. You could almost touch the atmosphere. If ever my throat felt dry at the start of a programme, this was the night, as I introduced proceedings to millions back home. And, more so than ever, it was imperative as a presenter to concentrate. My senses were being bombarded with voices in my ear from London and Rome plus the roar of the spectators all around. Then, of course, as always at an outside broadcast, I had to make sure I did not forget any of my memorised introduction. No autocue in those days at sporting events like that, although there often is now.

The final itself lived up to all expectations. The huge crowd went silent as the starter raised his pistol. Even in such an awesome arena, it was not difficult to pick out his lone voice barking at the fastest men on earth, on the brink of what turned out to be a record-breaking race. And then it was all over in less than ten seconds. Utterly explosive and inordinately thrilling. Ben Johnson the winner in a new world best of 9.83, with Carl Lewis second, Ray Stewart third and Linford Christie fourth. Glorious headlines followed a sensational encounter. Yet, the statistics today will tell you that Carl Lewis became champion with a new world record time of 9.93, and Linford Christie took the bronze. The bizarre aftermath occurred a year later at the Olympics in Seoul, where Ben Johnson won yet again, but failed a dope test. He was stripped of his Olympic Gold, his title from '87 was taken away and his world record revoked as well. He was kicked out of the sport for a time, returned unsuccessfully, failed another drugs test and was finally banned for life. Obviously, the memory of that epic Rome final is tarnished, but, at the time, it was a quite breathtaking contest and I prefer to remember the event itself and not the dismal postscript.

The following year came the Olympics, which ran through our night-time from Seoul in South Korea. Jim was out there, while I was in the studio in London, and it was Jim who reported to us live the dramatic events surrounding the disqualification of Ben Johnson. We had Olympic programmes scattered through the day, either on Channel 3 or Channel 4. Alison Holloway, former wife of comedian Jim Davidson, joined me as co-presenter on a two hour breakfast show on Channel 4 and I also returned later in the day for an early evening slot on ITV. Our presenting team also featured Dickie Davies, Elton Welsby, Hazel Irvine and, perhaps surprisingly but very efficiently, sport-loving film-buff Barry Norman, an inspired choice. I spent much of my spare time with European and Commonwealth 400 metres champion, Roger Black, who was recovering from a serious foot injury and had to get around on crutches. It kept him out of competition for the best part of two years and must have been very depressing for him, but he was terrific company. He obviously found his involvement fairly useful because he went on to become a highly-polished television presenter, as well as a motivational speaker. I interviewed scores of people during that Olympic fortnight and realised how much I was missing the chat show format I had enjoyed at TVam. Over the six years I was primarily working with ITV Sport, the emphasis increasingly focused on the event rather than the studio chat and this caused me immense frustration. I am not saying the decision was wrong - it made a lot of sense - but it often left me feeling unfulfilled after a snatched couple of minutes with some sporting luminary. When I first joined, there was scope for film features too, but that soon dropped off, not before a happy weekend in Barcelona with Gary Lineker and Mark Hughes, who were playing there at the time.

Inevitably, Gary was interviewed regularly during his successful years with England. He was always good value, but it is interesting to note he occasionally joined us at Midweek Sport Special just to watch the games we were covering and see how we handled things behind the scenes. No doubt he saw his future in the media even then, like Roger Black perhaps, and he was not a bad judge, was he? I recall one night when we were chatting about his and Michelle's new baby George. He said they were concerned about some lumps on his head and I ventured my layman's opinion that it was probably a case of the condition known as cradle cap. He said they reckoned it was more than that, but it was rather baffling. Only a few days later, as everyone knows, tests revealed six-week-old George had a form of leukaemia and there followed some desperately stressful times for the family with intensive treatment before, happily, he made a full recovery.

Midweek Sport Special was a highlights magazine programme which usually went out on Wednesdays with a range of top events, mainly football and boxing, but a smattering of others, including snooker and ice skating. On football nights, especially, you could walk around the editing suites to witness ever more feverish activity towards on-air time, as we cut down the various matches we had covered and decided which one deserved the greatest emphasis. In fact, Wednesday could be a very long day with script writing in the morning and afternoon, possibly pre-recording an interview and then rehearsals in the evening before the starting titles rolled at twenty to eleven. We would come off air around about midnight and then luxuriate in a lengthy wind-down with some amber neck-oil. I nearly always stayed at a nearby hotel, as did many of the team, because we started reasonably early the next day with a de-brief. Occasionally, we would be joined by Chris Tarrant returning from a gig somewhere and staying close to the Capital Radio studios in readiness for a crack-of-dawn start on his breakfast show. This tended to inflate the drinks bill somewhat.

Most of the football on television in those days went out as recorded highlights, but we were able to broadcast certain selected fixtures live and one I will not forget featured England against Brazil in the Rous Cup at Wembley. I introduced it live from the stadium and our half time scoop was an interview with the by-then-infamous Diego Maradona. It was less than a year after his nauseating hand-of-God goal against England in the Mexico World Cup – how on earth did the ref and linesman miss that? Inevitably, I wanted to ask him about it. Ossie Ardiles, with his halting English, acted as interpreter, but it was an utter waste of time. I have no idea how my questions sounded to Diego via Ossie and I would also like to know how much they colluded before the response made it back, but take it from me, he did not say, yes, sorry, old chap, I punched it in, I admit I am a naughty boy and I so wish we had let you win and go on to take the cup home!

Something mildly historic occurred in my life that day. Producer Trevor East and I arrived at the ground around lunchtime for the evening kick-off and, in the natural way of things before an important, potentially stressful outside broadcast, we both sensed the unseen hand beckoning us inexorably towards the gents. We took adjoining traps, with Trevor clutching his new toy...one of the world's first mobiles, about the size of a housebrick. Our cocoon of silent concentration was broken by the phone ringing and Trevor's answer to his secretary. "Hi, Hilary!........ Yes, he is........no, not far away at all....I'm sure he can....give me a moment." At which point, the high-tech housebrick came sliding under the partition and I spoke for the first time in my life on a mobile phone. Yes, sitting on the loo at Wembley Stadium, May 19th 1987. Sadly, the plaque will have gone now amid the rubble of the departed stadium. England drew one all, by the way, with our goal coming from a diving header by Gary Lineker in front of 92,000 fans.

David Pleat, who had become manager of Tottenham Hotspur after leaving Luton Town, was my guest pundit that day, one of many experts I was lucky enough to talk to during my time with ITV Sport. Kevin Keegan was a regular in the early days, but I think he found the travelling from his home in Spain a chore, especially as his close friend Brian Moore was no longer involved in the studio side of things. Brian Clough joined me for a few as well. Not surprisingly, he always said something that made you sit up and take notice, while Denis Law was also well worth listening to. For the World Cup in 1990, we had a terrific cast of former England internationals; Rodney Marsh, Emlyn Hughes, Geoff Hurst, Gordon Banks and, of course, Jimmy Greaves. In Italy itself, Elton Welsby and company were joined by Ian St. John, Ron Atkinson and Trevor Francis.

It was a superb tournament for England, of course, but desperately disappointing to fail on penalties in the semi-final against West Germany. If people had not appreciated him before, they certainly came to recognise the genius of Paul Gascoigne in the summer of 1990. As a football fan, I feel cheated, as I did with George Best in a previous generation, that we never enjoyed more subsequent years of Gazza at his best. What a waste!

For that dramatic semi-final in Turin, I had Geoff, Gordon, and Jimmy with me and we all suffered shared anguish on and off-air, as those vital penalties sailed high into the night sky. What a tortuous time it was for England manager Bobby Robson, who received so much criticism during his tenure and aged visibly in the spotlight. He was always an utter gentleman to deal with, though, and is rightly regarded as one of the most amiable guys in the game. I also have a high regard for his successor in the job, Graham Taylor. I spent a considerable amount of time with him during Italia 90, but had known him for some years before. Indeed, we ended up alongside each other at an Ashes Test match at Lord's and together enjoyed a typically attractive innings from David Gower, who fell just fourteen short of his century.

In idle moments during that World Cup, our production assistants made up an anagram football team of ITV's line-up. Among them Elly Wetnobs (Elton Welsby), Emry Hard Ons (Rodney Marsh), Nora No Stink (Ron Atkinson), V.E. Arsetrot (Trevor East), Sir C.N. Overfart (Trevor Francis), Jan Noshit (Ian St. John), Jil T.H. Noseram (Jim Rosenthal) and Marge S.Vimjey (Jimmy Greaves). I came out as Nice Wonk (gosh, that was close!) and our director Pat Mordecai mutated into Erica D. Moaticrapi. Good to know we were all working hard behind the scenes! I am glad to say, incidentally, that Jil. T.H. Noseram and I smoothed out any difficulties between us years ago now.

Covering Ice Skating Championships gave me the chance to visit some fascinating cities, such as Budapest, Prague and Sarajevo. In the beautiful and historic city of Leningrad (St. Petersburg), we had to move hotels after the first night because many of us had glass missing from our bedroom windows. We woke up the following day with a couple of inches of snow on the carpet! We were always beautifully looked after by local guides, who wanted to make sure we showed their countries in the best possible light, but Prague was a little daunting because we knew the KGB were keeping an eye on us. We were hardly a threat to world peace, but we were often aware of dodgy-looking heavies hovering in the vicinity. The truth of it was revealed when we palled up with a couple of switchboard girls from our hotel. They asked us our room numbers and assured us all we were OK. What did they mean by that? They said words to the effect that all rooms on the twelfth floor were bugged and any others ending in the numbers four or ten! If they really wanted to know your inside leg measurement, they would make sure you were booked into one of those.

The holiday programme Wish You Were Here? came from the same stable as Thames Sport, so I was roped in for a few trips and I was hardly going to complain. Close to home, I enjoyed a somewhat rain-sozzled cruise down the River Shannon amongst quite captivating scenery in Southern Ireland and a tranquil sojourn at a country club on the banks of Loch Lomond in Scotland. Twenty-one miles long and up to five miles wide, Loch Lomond is surrounded by mountain peaks and spectacularly beautiful. We filmed the length of it by helicopter, an outing I strongly recommend. The programme also sent me to the Dominican Republic, Corfu and, most memorably, a Mediterranean cruise of historic sites to include Italy, Egypt, the Holy Land, Asia Minor and Greece. Right up my street. The cruise itself was the last word in luxury, as far as I was concerned, but the excursions on land really took some beating. All for the first time, I saw the awesome remains of Pompeii, the pyramids near Cairo, and the places in Bethlehem and Jerusalem that had hitherto just been names, albeit highly significant ones, in the Bible. We also visited Ephesus on the Turkish coast, a magnificent reminder of how things must have been during the height of the Roman Empire. While there, we were told by our guide the rather grizzly tale of the men's public toilets. Nobles used to carry out their business over a long row of stone-built receptacles. Slaves used to clean their masters afterwards with a sponge. To show his devotion, one of the slaves is alleged to have swallowed his master's used sponge. This appears to have been a gross error of judgement and the bottom line, I am afraid, is that he choked to death.

My years at ITV Sport were tough for commercial television generally. The recession was biting deeply by the end of the eighties, so much so that we ended our contracts for ice skating, gymnastics and ultimately athletics. All of these had a direct bearing on me as presenter, as did a later decision to withdraw from snooker, another sport I hosted – and much enjoyed – for ITV. One way or another I was missing the broader world of current affairs and topical magazine programmes and feeling increasingly hemmed in by sport. A huge chunk of what I was doing had disappeared and, as I said earlier, the emphasis was more on the action than the links and interviewing. On top of that, Central and Granada wanted to break away to cover their own local football matches in midweek. They felt we showed too much of a London bias. A phone call from Anne Diamond's husband Mike Hollingsworth looked like giving me just the opportunity I needed. He told me he had been asked to produce a mid-morning magazine programme for the BBC and wanted to get Anne and me together again. The one possible drawback, he said, was that it would be coming from Birmingham, so we would all have to move, but I was perfectly happy to head back to the Midlands where I knew so many people and had such terrific memories. It was far from being a done deal, but Anne rang me a couple of weeks later saying it looked odds-on and she was really excited about it. At about this time, Thames Television was losing its franchise to Carlton, so my immediate future with ITV Sport was uncertain anyway. I was greatly relieved at the prospect of linking up with Anne again and doing what I felt I did best. What followed was undoubtedly the happiest time of my broadcasting career. Six hundred shows over four years which, despite constant antagonism from the press, attracted audiences of up to fifteen million a week.

Chapter Eleven

PROTECTING A HERO

The life of a freelance in any occupation can be precarious, but the plus side for me has always been the variety. During my time concentrating largely on sport, I became involved in a range of other programmes. For instance, I spent a weekend at Gatwick with Fern Britton, co-hosting five live shows from the airport over a Bank Holiday weekend. It was a fascinating behind-the-scenes look at the workings of a major airport, a forerunner to some extent of all the fly-on-the-wall series that have proved so popular in later years. I also stood in frequently for Mike Scott on The Time, The Place, the morning chat show with a studio audience that mirrored Kilroy on the other side. That programme had been Mike's idea and he presented it for many years before he retired and John Stapleton took over as his permanent replacement. I have also guested on numerous game shows, about twenty-five at the last count, from Blankety Blank to Family Fortunes, and from Wipeout to the Weakest Link.

The Weakest Link with Anne Robinson was the most recent and it was certainly an experience and a half! Pitted against each other in this particular show were nine people who had first made the headlines in the eighties. Standing either side of me under the withering glare of Cruella de Bile were actress Su Pollard and pop star Limahl. Also in the line-up were ex-page three girl Linda Lusardi, singer Toyah Wilcox, darts champion Eric Bristow, Maggie Thatcher impersonator Steve Nallon, society photographer Normski plus Bob Carolgees and Spit the Dog. The Queen of Mean suggested on the programme that I had lost rather a lot of hair since my breakfast television days, but that bit failed to make the edited version. A number of my fellow contestants and I went a long way back, though clearly not as far back as my hair. Steve Nallon was an early faller and

Normski did not last too long either. Bob and Spit were hilarious, but also left the party quite early, Toyah looked good for a long time, but, after nearly three gruelling hours rooted to the same spot, just Linda and I remained. She had brought the house down earlier when Anne was asking her with that cutting way of hers what exactly she was doing with her time these days. "Well, Anne," replied Linda, "I've got two little ones." Not from where I was standing she hadn't! The audience also loved a response of Eric's earlier in the show. "So, Eric," she leered. "You live in Leek. Why?" "Because that's where my house is, Anne!" Brilliant! Linda got the better of me in the penultimate round, but somehow the questions went my way in the final straight. My classical education paid dividends big-time just when I needed it, as Anne delivered the killer question. "What is the common term for the medical expression tinea pedis?" Yes, yes, yes. I've had it on and off for years! Such an attractive condition! "Athlete's foot," I shouted in triumph and landed over six grand for my favourite charity, St. Mary's Hospice in Birmingham. I was thrilled. I have never won anything in my life, apart from the parents' egg-and-spoon race at my children's school and then I failed the dope test afterwards.

The Krypton Factor was demanding in a rather different way. Four ITV Olympic presenters were invited on as a prelude to the Olympic Games of 1988. Hosted by Gordon Burns, who is currently my opposite number in Manchester, presenting North West Tonight for the BBC, the show put us through our paces, both mentally and physically. The ITV team of Alison Holloway, Dickie Davies, Elton Welsby and myself competed with four former Olympic medallists. We spent two days with Granada Television in Manchester, first of all filming the cerebral stuff in the studio, before the real test up on the moors and that infamous assault course. They staged eliminators on the course before a two-a-side final. David Wilkie, breast-stroke gold medallist from Montreal in '76 and sprinter Sonia Lannaman, who won bronze in Moscow in 1980 against Elton and me. Two still superfit Olympians against a pair of creaky, coiffured presenters! That course is a killer. After a gentle-ish start, it just gets tougher and tougher until your legs become dead weights for the closing stages. David Wilkie streaked home in first place, while I somehow managed to finish second after overhauling Elton shortly before the water jump. Overall, the presenters did enough to beat the medallists and win the show. That was not the end of my day, though. Thames Television were staging a high-profile summer party in the afternoon on the banks of the river in central London and wanted me there. Granada agreed to provide a helicopter to fly me south from the Pennines, roughly down the line of the M6 and M1 to the playing fields behind my home in Berkhamsted. Thence a fast car took the family and me to the party, where I paraded alongside the so-called faces of Thames television, including Benny Hill and Eamonn Andrews.

Sporting Triangles gave me the chance to present a game show myself. It first surfaced when I was still with TVam, based on an idea from the comedian and broadcaster Don MacLean. My old colleague Gary Newbon, Head of Sport at Central, invited me to be the quizmaster in a game that involved three teams of two players. The two resident captains were old friends, Olympic gold medallist Tessa Sanderson and Jimmy Greaves, and we started with one visiting skipper each week, which soon became Andy Gray on a regular basis. It was fairly hi-tech for those days, which did not suit me at all, and, during the show itself, my brain was addled with what the new-fangled device called a computer was doing. It was a forerunner really of all today's glitzy, technology-dominated shows, but, at that time, it used to drive us all mad because it kept breaking down and we had to put up with lengthy delays while it was sorted out. We seemed to wait ages for that infernal electronic dice to roll, telling us what subject the next question would be. Incidentally, I received quite a few letters from viewers about the word dice. I said, 'Roll the dice' frequently and I was pulled up for using the plural, when I should have said, 'Roll the DIE' because there was only one. Yes, I know that was strictly correct, but it would have sounded utterly ridiculous, don't you think?

I know now, looking back, that I did not cope very well with the early shows and the critics felt the same! "Why is Nick Owen such a cross-patch?" asked a writer in the Mirror called Pratt. Well, anyone who knows me will tell you that I am not, but the programme tended to be such a feat of concentration at times it must have looked like that. There were still some lively and hilarious moments, particularly in the second series, when we had all warmed up a bit and the whole structure had been streamlined. Tessa struggled a bit with her all-round sporting knowledge and seemed to come third rather more often than she would have liked. I remember one time Jeff Farmer, our producer, decided to help her a little during the commercial break. He told her that the mystery face she would be seeing at the start of the second half would be the goalkeeper Paul Barron. I was in on the fact that she had been tipped off so, when I posed the question, I was confident she would be off to a flying start for part two. "So who is it, Tess? "I asked. Back came the reply, no hesitation: "John Burridge." Groans from the production gallery in my ear and I nearly feel off my chair.

We would usually record two shows in an evening and I have to confess I was barely up to speed on one occasion after attending the birth of our third son Chris at four o'clock that morning. He was born at the RAF Halton Hospital near Wendover in Buckinghamshire, not far from our home. I am proud to say I have been there for the birth of all our four children, although if you had asked me about it, say, thirty years ago I would have said no way! I am dreadfully squeamish, but I am sure all parents will agree that the sheer beauty and magic of the moment transcends all normal inhibitions. For me, it has to be the ultimate experience to see your own child come into the world. Painful for Mum, stressful and tearful for both of us, but what an overwhelming occasion!

Two years later, Jenny was born at the same hospital and I shudder even now to think how close we came to losing her. She arrived comfortably enough (NB! Man speaking here!), but, as she lay in Jill's arms, I noticed our longed-for first little girl turning blue. I alerted the midwife and, within moments, it was clear she had inhaled a quantity of mucus. She could not breathe. The midwife pressed a button on the wall and alarm bells rang around the hospital. Within seconds, our small delivery room was packed with white coats, as doctors tried desperately to suck the mucus out of her lungs with a straw. Jill and I could only sit and anxiously watch the frenetic activity surrounding her tiny incubator. After what seemed an age, but was probably only a few minutes, she started to breathe normally again, we all let out a cheer and Jill and I burst into tears.

Back in November 1986, however, after the huge emotion of Chris's arrival, I raced home for a couple of hours' sleep before heading to Birmingham to record another two editions of Sporting Triangles at Central TV. I felt utterly drained. To his credit, Gary Newbon made a big fuss of me with the studio audience and wheeled on the champagne for all involved in the show to celebrate with me.

We were sometimes getting audiences of up to fourteen million. Gary and Jeff brought in a gag-writer to help Jim and me along with our banter. His name was Barry Roberts, an ex-fireman forced out of the brigade by injury. A Scouser with a cutting line in humour, Barry has written scripts for radio comedy shows, supplied Greavesie and me with numerous gags over the years and made, I hope, a tidy living as an after-dinner speaker. He is certainly very funny to listen to. Although the show seemed reasonably successful, I always sensed that Gary was wondering if I was the right man for the job. I admit I had taken time to settle into what was the comparatively foreign world of light entertainment, but I did feel I was bedding down OK. However, through no fault of my own, another problem emerged which did not help my case at all.

Tessa Sanderson told me she wanted an agent and asked if she could meet mine. I said he was coming that night and, indeed, I was able to introduce her to Paul Vaughan that same evening in the hospitality room. Apparently, someone took offence at this. Don't ask me how or why, because it seems amazing to me that anyone could be offended by a quiet business chat happening across a room. Even so, Gary rang me at home the next day to say some people had been upset by Paul and Tessa talking business in the green room and would I ask Paul not to do it again. Well, Paul was far from amused when I told him, not surprisingly in my opinion, and insisted they had chatted only briefly before agreeing to link up on the phone later in the week. After all, Tessa had asked to see him. Tessa confirmed all this to me only recently and also assured me that their chat was extremely brief on the night. The next thing I knew was that Paul had had heated exchanges with Gary and with Bob Southgate, then Controller of Factual Programmes at Central Television. There was talk of litigation and it struck me then that, whatever my plus or minus points in presenting Sporting Triangles, Bob and Gary would not be too keen on employing a Paul Vaughan man from then on.

However, I was still hoping to be involved with the promised next series, when Paul's office received a call about my possibly hosting another national game show, Hitman, for TVS, who were based in Southampton. Peter Plant, then working with Paul, told them that I was already committed to Triangles. TVS decided to approach Andy Craig, who was an established and popular presenter with Central's regional news programme in the East Midlands. Andy told them he was unable to take up their offer because he was doing the next series of......Sporting Triangles. TVS went back to Peter Plant. Did he know that Andy Craig was hosting the next series of Sporting Triangles? No, he did not. And that was how we first heard about it.

Bob Southgate wrote to me apologising for the way I had learned about my fate. ... "whoever was or was not to blame, it is obviously disturbing to you personally to learn all of this through rumour." He went on, "I am sorry about the events of last week and I am sorry too that we shall not be seeing you in the programme next time around. Perhaps you would let me take this opportunity of thanking you for all the very hard work you put in and in particular for the professional way in which you tackled the job and got on with all the panel members. I hope that we will have an opportunity of working together on other projects in the future and I wish you well with all your current undertakings." This was August 1988 and those undertakings included the Olympic Games due to start any time. Not great for the confidence, as one ITV company very publicly sacks the man who is soon going to lead the station's coverage of the world's biggest sporting event.

Peter had received a letter from Bob and had a telephone conversation with him. One paragraph, I think, explains what Bob had implied to him and how reluctantly, but diplomatically, Peter accepted his reasoning for kicking me out. "Despite strong suggestions to the contrary, Nick and I accept that your decision was based on the very detailed research which was carried out on the programme, together with the conclusion that he is personally identified by the viewing public with sport and with sport alone, so that his appearances on Sporting Triangles are not effective. We are deeply sorry that his identification with sport has become a handicap. Both Nick and I trust your judgement and appreciate that you chose the best presenter on merit. It is, of course, with sorrow that Nick feels he must accept that he is not the best presenter and that, for the sake of the success of the series, he must stand down in favour of another." Bob Southgate had also told me in his letter that seeing me off was one of a number of changes they were making. It later emerged that Liverpool and England football hero Emlyn Hughes was coming in to replace Tessa Sanderson as a team captain. He had been enormously successful as a captain on the BBC's A Question of Sport, so it was a huge coup for Central. My departure was revealed at the press conference announcing the signing of Emlyn. My story hit the tabloid newspapers in a big way, with reports of the first knock-back for the so-called golden boy of television. I was shattered by it and deeply disappointed at the way we found out. I think all the main players involved were deeply embarrassed about it, particularly as I had been a close colleague of theirs for some considerable time, when I worked solely for Central. I had agreed to present Hitman for TVS and that was to be given as the reason for my going, but it never turned out like that. Gary made it clear I had been axed and implied I was on television far too much. Yes, I had been fronting Triangles at eight o'clock on a Wednesday evening and then returning for Midweek Sport Special after News at Ten, but it was nothing like the overkill you get with some presenters these days. For a long time after that, I found it hard to share a room with Gary Newbon.

Sporting Triangles continued for two more series after my two and then it was pulled by ITV. It was Thames TV who made the decision to drop Triangles from their schedules as they operated the national airwaves during the week. It was rumoured that they had made the move in retaliation for Central's decision, along with Granada, to go it alone with midweek sport. Tit-for-tat, as it were. I had long gone from Sporting Triangles by then so I could not possibly comment.

As for Hitman, that was terrific fun to make at the TVS studios in Maidstone, produced and directed by Graham C. Williams. It was basically a test of memory for the people who took part. They were shown a film and had to ask questions about it afterwards. The films themselves were extremely informative and well put together, so it made for an interesting programme, as well as entertaining. What made it stand out, though, was the money on offer to the winner. The biggest cash prize in British quiz show history....all of £3,000! Hard to believe now, but that was breathtaking at the time. The show went out in the daytime and did fairly well in the ratings. It was hampered by the fact it was split-network, which meant it was shown all over the country, but at different times. For whatever reason, programme planners decided not to commission another series, which I believe is a pity because it was a good format. As time has shown over and over again, programmes of all sorts often need more than one series to settle down and build an audience.

I started this chapter talking about the variety in life as a freelance. The quiz show experience was not the end of it. After someone's late withdrawal, I received a last minute call-up to join the panel of judges for Miss World 1986! Luckily, no research required. I was at the offices of Thames Television at the time, so I had my dinner suit sent there from home and hurtled off to the Royal Albert Hall. My fellow judges included boxing champion Lloyd Honeyghan and tennis star John Lloyd and, after much negotiating behind the scenes, we came up with Miss Trinidad and Tobago as our winner. The audience across the globe that night was estimated at a tidy 700 million.

I also fronted a number of film premieres, Royal or otherwise, during my time with Thames. They were always an enjoyable diversion from sport and enabled me to see a little inside the world of the movie business. I fronted programmes for a couple of James Bond films, Licence to Kill and Living Daylights, and cherish memories of a hugely entertaining lunch with the great producer Cubby Broccoli and his daughter, Barbara. I was lucky enough to get on the set of a Bond movie at Pinewood and enjoyed interviewing the stars, including the Bond of the time, Timothy Dalton. The actress Lois Maxwell, who had played the original Miss Moneypenny, joined me as co-host for the Licence to Kill programme. We were due on air at nine o'clock in the evening, so we had to record our opening links in the Leicester Odeon foyer long before there was anyone else there. To give it a feeling of bustling activity, our producer Steve Minchin hired a load of extras to mill around in the background in their dinner suits. The interviewing of VIP guests had barely finished before the actual show began to be transmitted. Steve and company were editing parts two and three when part one was actually going out. It kept them regular for weeks. Three other premieres stick in my mind. Madame Sousatska, for which I interviewed Shirley MacLaine and joined her at the party afterwards; Labyrinth, co-hosted with Anne Diamond, when we spoke to David Bowie, and Back to the Future, which gave me the chance to drive that mean magic machine of a car they used to travel through time.

It also meant more contact with Royalty, particularly Princess Diana. She had always been a fan of TVam and often sent us messages through Richard Dalton, the hairdresser she shared with Anne Diamond. I first met the Princess at a charity function in September 1985. Her lady-in-waiting, Anne Beckwith-Smith, came across to me, saying the Princess had heard I was there and wanted to be introduced. Great, except that I was in the middle of a ferocious nosebleed! I stuck a piece of tissue up my conk and went over for an extremely nasal conversation in which I dare not look down, in case the blood started to surge again. We chatted about my back troubles, our children and how our regular contributor on TVam, the gossip columnist Nigel Dempster, was the bane of her life. It was at her instigation that I was asked to host an awards ceremony alongside her not long afterwards, but, as I said earlier, after the Pamela Stephenson incident, I had to pull out. However, there were many other opportunities later and I greatly enjoyed meeting and chatting to her. One time, when we had been together about three times in six days, she asked, "Are you following me around, or am I following you?"
I replied, "People will talk."
She came back, "I don't mind!"
I said, "Well, nor do I!"

At one Royal Premiere, she was moving down the line talking to stars of the film and VIP guests, when she and Prince Charles alighted on the actress, Lynda Bellingham. I had recorded most of my introductions and interviews for the programme by then, so I was hovering in the shadows nearby. I heard Princess Diana say to Lynda, "Where's Nick?" and Lynda pointed in my direction with the words, "He's over there". To everyone's amazement amid the regal hush, Diana looked over, shouted out, "Hi, Nick", waved and carried on. Prince Charles looked totally bewildered.

She was our special guest in October 1989 at a Sports Awards ceremony Thames Television staged over lunch at the Café Royal. It was also the occasion of the impressionist Mike Yarwood's comeback after two very lean years, when he had almost disappeared from our screens. He had suffered from well-documented alcohol problems and panic attacks. He was desperately nervous to be returning at such a high profile event in the presence of Princess Diana. Producer John D. Taylor had invited him to perform because he was known to have an excellent impression of Prince Charles up his sleeve. He was noticeably nervous at our table and, just as I was about to introduce him on stage, we realised he had disappeared. Our production team found him in the toilets and it was some little time before he was coaxed to the microphone. I am afraid to say his performance was very disappointing and he knew it at the time. "A fine comeback this is turning out to be," he proclaimed rather sadly from the stage. Among the four hundred guests was comedian Frank Carson. He shouted rather cruelly, "Even I am funnier than Mike Yarwood." It was acutely uncomfortable for us all. The Sun newspaper's first edition led with it the following day. "Yarwood flops in front of Di". Our recorded highlights of the ceremony went out the same evening. The awards themselves had overrun and needed more time than expected in the final version, but it must still have been mortifying for Mike that his whole act was edited out.

One of the great benefits of being in the public eye is getting the opportunity to play football or cricket alongside some great sporting stars of yesteryear. I turned out regularly for the ATV All Stars football team back in the late seventies and the line-up would often be a real who's who of sport and showbiz. Jasper Carrott and Led Zeppelin singer Robert Plant regularly led the forward line, we had comedian and broadcaster Don Maclean in midfield as well as Trevor Oakes of Showaddywaddy, while Bev Bevan helped stiffen up the back four, if you will pardon the expression. Just to make sure we had some real footballing skill in the side, we often had that great double act of Ron Atkinson and Jim Smith in defence, with the quality of Alan Hinton and Bruce Rioch, for instance, making us tick in midfield. I remember one match I slipped the ball to Bruce Rioch at least forty yards out. The former Luton legend (that's how I see him anyway, despite his years with Aston Villa, Derby, Everton and Scotland) cracked it home with his magnificent left boot. I just could not wait to get home and ring my father about that one. I took all the credit, of course, for setting him up.

Just prior to the FA Cup Final at Wembley in 1987, I played in a special celebrity match before the real event between Coventry and Tottenham Hotspur. I had slightly more pace than Jimmy Tarbuck, David Frost and snooker's Steve Davis, but was hardly equipped to compete with Daley Thompson, Bobby Moore and Mike Channon! Quite an experience to play in front of more than ninety thousand people!

I am still playing charity cricket, largely for the Bunbury team, a creation of the self-confessed loon, David English. Amongst his many claims to fame, David has been manager of the Bee Gees and Eric Clapton. He has raised no less than eight million pounds over the years for charity and grass-roots cricket and fully deserved his MBE in 2003. Amongst his many achievements, he founded the annual English Schools Cricket Association Under-Fifteen Festival. An astonishing statistic this: ninety five per cent of all England Test cricketers since 1986 have played in that festival. The entire England squad in the successful tour of the West Indies in 2004 came through the festival. David is one of the most charismatic characters you will ever meet, with an astonishing capacity to tell the same joke a hundred times and still make it hilarious. It was something else, though, that made us both chuckle at a dinner not so long ago at my old school Shrewsbury, where they were staging the under-fifteen cricket festival which he inspired. The Minister for Sport, Richard Caborn, delivered the keynote speech to youngsters and officials and made a point of thanking the sponsors, Weetabix. Just a pity, the actual benefactors had their name emblazoned on huge banners around the hall....Shredded Wheat!

I tend not to bat very often, though I did feature once in a stand of 34 with the former West Indies captain Jimmy Adams. He scored 33 of them and the other one was a leg bye, but it was MY leg. My bowling is usually fairly generous to the other side and remarkably short of pace. In fact, it is so slow that, if I am not happy with a delivery, I can catch it up before it gets to the other end and bring it back. Bunbury aficionados still talk with respect of a breathtaking catch I took left-handed on the boundary to dismiss England opener Nick Knight, when he was on the threshold of a dashing century on a steaming hot afternoon at Atherstone in Warwickshire. It was suggested mischievously by some that I had decided to wave at someone on the far side of the ground at just the right time. Later that day, as I struggled with the bat, Warwickshire's Dougie Brown cruelly inquired as to whether I would like a bell in the ball. I was invited by Bob Willis to play in one game at Stoke D'Abernon in Surrey with, amongst others, Bob himself, Gary Lineker, the former England fast bowler John Lever and the mighty Geoff Hurst. What made it memorable for me was that Geoff did not have an abdominal protector, as they are officially called. In other words, a box. And whose did he borrow? Yes, you have guessed it - the only man ever to have scored a hat-trick in a World Cup Final wore my box. Awesome! And that, my friends, is the closest I have ever been to sporting greatness.

A host of familiar faces as Derek Jameson, renowned Fleet Street editor, marries Ellen. Judith Chalmers, Gloria Hunniford and Su Pollard are there, plus David Hamilton and Nick Ross. But who is the bridesmaid in picture on the left? Surely not the Queen of Mean?

Disneyland with Jackie Collins and Patrick Duffy.

Meeting a true legend of the screen. With Sophia Loren.

In the garden with Bob Hope. A very special experience.

The funniest man of all time and a Luton Town supporter to boot!

*After a helicopter flight to the party, lining up with Bandmaster Benny Hill,
Tim Brooke-Taylor, Lionel Blair, Richard Briers, Eamonn Andrews, George
Layton, Bernie Winters and Jim Davidson.*

*Some of the Olympics team of 1988. Can you spot some of the faces? They
include Roger Black, Sue Barker, Harvey Smith, Elton Welsby, Allan Wells,
Alison Holloway, Dickie Davies, Hazel Irvine, Jim Watt, Suzanne Dando,
Alan Pascoe and Duncan Goodhew.*

Braving the agonies of a slipped disc, trumpeting my first ever visit to Scotland.

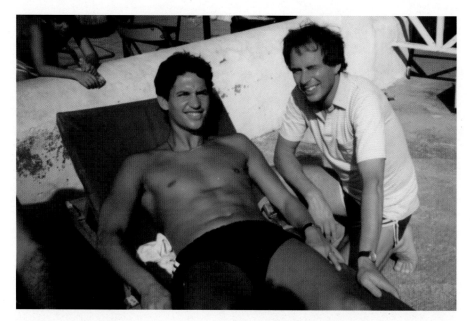

It's a hard life being a sports reporter! A working life in Barcelona with Gary Lineker, almost done to a crisp.

Soaking up the sun with Gary Lineker and Mark Hughes.

The eternal struggle to look like a human.

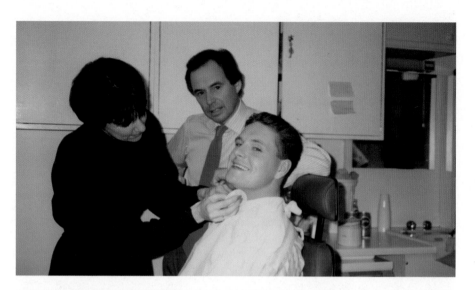

Supervising make-up for Paul Gascoigne before an appearance on Midweek Sport Special.

The line-up for the big match before the big match in 1987 when Coventry beat Spurs. Back row includes Ronnie Corbett, referee Jack Taylor, Nick Berry, John Birt, Jimmy Tarbuck, Lloyd Honeyghan, Chris Quentin, Greg Dyke, Daley Thompson and myself. In the front row, Bobby Moore, Steve Davis, Steve Cram, Michael Le Vell, Dennis Waterman, Mike Channon, Adam Woodyatts, and Steven Pinder.

Commentating on the World Cup in 1982.

A picture of which I am particularly proud – with the Littlewoods Cup after Luton won it in 1988.

Andy and Tim meet new brother Chris for the first time, as I headed off to present Sporting Triangles.

Chris, not yet two, obviously unaware that he, Andy and Tim were in the presence of a Superstar!

Jenny and Chris.

Oldest son Andy bowling here alongside Graeme Hick.

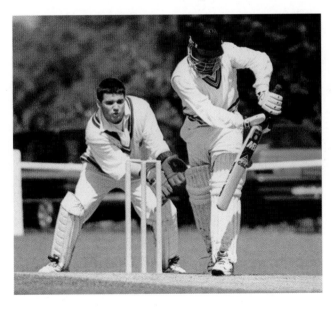

Son Tim wicket-keeping for West Bromwich Dartmouth in the Birmingham League.

Presenting Airport '90 with Fern Britton.

The hardships of the Dominican Republic – Wish you were Here?

Trying to look cool at the premiere of Back to the Future in Leicester Square.

Early hints of a stomach during filming for 'Wish you were Here?' in Corfu.

Sports Awards with Princess Diana. Colleague Keith Mosedale looks particularly excited in the background.

My screen wife of many years and never a cross word. With Anne in the early 90s.

With Greg Dyke and Jasper Carrott, little knowing about the crisis soon to befall Greg.

Cassandra Harris and Pierce Brosnan with Anne and me at their wonderful seaside home in Malibu.

Recreating my wonder catch to dismiss Nick Knight.

*My esteemed colleagues on Midlands
Today. Shefali Oza, Suzanne Virdee
and Steve Clamp.*

The showbiz life with David Essex.

*Just what was going through my father's mind, as we stood on the beach at
Dunkirk, 60 years after his dramatic escape?*

Chapter Twelve

CAPTIVE AUDIENCE

Joan Collins was the first guest on Good Morning with Anne and Nick when it launched at Pebble Mill in October 1992. The Owen family had moved back to Birmingham in the summer and, in many ways, it was terrific to be back. Jill felt more at home, the children soon became settled in their schools and enjoyed all the facilities readily available in a city compared with a small country town. Inevitably, I have a special feeling for the Pebble Mill studios because it was there that I started my broadcasting career. In little over thirty years, the name Pebble Mill has become synonymous across the land with high profile programmes on BBC television and radio in Birmingham. The ever popular Archers on sound plus TV shows, including Angels, Poldark, All Creatures Great and Small, Howards' Way, Brothers, Dalziel and Pascoe, Pebble Mill at One and many, many more have all come from the same building. It is a mystery to many how the BBC can readily relinquish such a well-established brand name and move to new premises in the centre of the city.

I hope that the Anne and Nick show left its mark too with six hundred live programmes over four years, starting, as I said, with Joan Collins, who arrived in a stunning black leather suit. She looked fantastic, but the details are all a bit of a blur now because I was so nervous at the time. I distinctly remember that Anne had to do much of the talking in the first ten minutes or so, as I calmed down. It did not help much that Joan only joined us on set while the title music was playing, so we had no chance to have a chat beforehand. I usually like to build a hint of a relationship with guests before kick-off, if I have not met them on previous occasions, so we are not complete strangers when we first talk on air. Joan, then approaching sixty, was a terrific guest, though, and she stayed with us for the whole programme, the best part of two hours. She joined in our interview with Coronation Street actor Roy Barraclough, asked a question of our resident doctor Mark Porter, making his television debut, and answered questions from viewers who had phoned in. Barbara Cartland appeared on that first show, predictably a vision in shocking pink, Cliff Richard sang a song, Will Hanrahan investigated hairdressing disasters and we looked at the dancing boom in connection with the release that week of the new film, "Strictly Ballroom." We also chatted to a company director from Oxford who had been driven to distraction by the constant screeching of his next door neighbour's parrot. In the end, he became so incensed he stormed round to their aviary in the garden and wrung the parrot's neck. He landed in court and was fined £600. With a rich bouquet of flowers for Joan, our first Anne and Nick came to an end.

Our boss was Anne's then-husband, Mike Hollingsworth. They had been together on and off since 1979, a stormy relationship, to say the least. He was an excellent editor, full of innovative ideas, and uncannily good at spotting talent. He was also very hard to please, with the occasional bursts of temper that were frightening to behold. One particular female presenter friend of mine was devastated by what he said to her about her face. He could reduce people to tears. When he and Anne fell out, they would sometimes barely talk to each other for weeks. I remember he would sometimes come into us and ask if the presenters were doing this or that, but only looking at me. One time, he called me into his office to get me to ask Anne if she was going to parents' evening that week! The beginning of Good Morning with Anne and Nick came only fifteen months after they had lost their little boy Sebastian to cot death. I had met Supi, as they affectionately called him, a few times in his short life and he was totally engaging as his brothers Oliver and Jamie had been before him. I heard the awful news via ITN on the morning of Oliver's birthday. Jill and I were due at their house in Camden the next day for his party. I simply could not believe what I was hearing and immediately rang up. I spoke first to Mike and then to Anne before calling Jill at work. Of course, we were shattered and found the funeral in Bournemouth, where Anne's parents lived, terribly moving. Before the service, when friends and family were gathering at her parents' bungalow, Anne invited Jill and me into a bedroom. There we saw little Supi lying in his white coffin. Jill had expected it. I had not and it was a big shock. What we saw took my breath away and I could barely speak. It was absolutely choking. He looked quite perfect, a little china doll peacefully at sleep. I will never forget that enormously poignant moment. The sight of Mike later, walking into church carrying that tiny coffin, was utterly wretched. They had asked me to give a reading at the service and I felt honoured to do so. Jill found a poem by Albert Midlane that seemed absolutely right.

> There's a friend for little children
> Above the bright blue sky,
> A friend who never changes,
> Whose love will never die;
> Our earthly friends may fail us,
> And change with changing years,
> This friend is always worthy
> Of that dear name he bears.
>
> There's a home for little children
> Above the bright blue sky,
> Where Jesus reigns in glory,
> A home of peace and joy;
> No home on earth is like it,
> Nor can with it compare;
> And everyone is happy,
> Nor could be happier there.

I am not religious, but I hope the family and friends gathered there were able to find some comfort in those evocative words. I was desperately anxious to read the piece without my voice breaking and I somehow achieved it, but the moment I was back in my pew I cannot deny I broke down and sobbed. Anne and Mike went on to have two more lovely little boys, Jake and Connor, during the time of Good Morning with Anne and Nick and, of course, she campaigned tirelessly, famously and successfully to cut down the cot death rate.

For my part, it was wonderful to be working alongside Anne again and I hope the new start helped both of them cope in some small way with their grief, which was still painfully raw. Anne had moved back to her old home territory of the Midlands and the three of us were embarking on a new series. Just to make us feel more at home, we were re-united with a favourite director from TVam, Bob Merrilees, and, during the next four years, under Mike Hollingsworth or his successor, Tessa Finch, we enjoyed some terrific experiences, some riotous and some very moving.

Nearly all of us shed a tear on a January day in 1993 when we helped complete the re-union of seven brothers and sisters who had been separated shortly before the Second World War. Their parents within a short time of each other in 1938 and the children were sent to an orphanage. The four boys and three girls were immediately split up into same-sex buildings and that was the last time the boys and girls saw of each other for years. They were 'distributed' for fostering or adoption and lost all contact. Peggy, one of the oldest, told us that the orphanage held dreadful memories for her, like something from Oliver Twist. She remembered sneaking into the kitchens once after the staff had eaten salmon. They had discarded the skin, but she devoured it with relish. "It was delicious," she said and she still loved salmon skin. It was Peggy who started the search for her brothers and sisters in the seventies. She discovered they came from Stafford and she went to a phone box from her home in the Potteries, armed with a mound of sixpences, to ring the children's department at Staffordshire County Council. She found George, he had previously made contact with Peter and slowly, but surely, the jigsaw took shape. On the day of our programme, Rosemarie, who had been a baby when they were sent to an orphanage, met Peter for the first time since the war. It made us all gulp as he walked on to Rosemarie's embrace. They held hands for the rest of the interview. Brother John, we learned, had died and sister Betty had been too overwhelmed by the turn of events to be able to join us. There was still one final reunion. Harry proved a problem to track down, until the local newspaper in Stoke-on-Trent ran a feature which prompted a call from a lady called Lilly. She told them she had been nursing

Harry. Harry, it emerged, had been born with a cleft palate and, amazing as it sounds today, he had been sent to an institution....for more than fifty years. Nurse Lilly brought him into the studio and some of his brothers and sisters had not seen him since before the war. It was remarkably moving to hear that Harry had not spoken for years, but he lost his shyness and started speaking clearly again after talking on the phone to Peter. The nurses at his home had been astounded. Peter told us, "The last time I saw Harry, I was about 14 and he was five. He hadn't learned to walk. I never saw him again until now. They didn't bother in those days." Anne could barely get the words out for her tears. "I cannot believe that fifty five years after you were split up as little children you are all together again for the first time. It's marvellous!" And there they were. Five of the seven, with Rosemarie holding Harry so very close to her, and all yearning to make up for those lost years. Finally, I said, "Make sure you give our love to Betty" and a highly emotional episode came to a close.

We were very proud of our small contribution to the plight of desperately traumatised children in Rwanda. In 1994, the most appalling systematic slaughter of men, women and children broke out as a result of vicious rivalry between the Hutu and Tutsi tribes. The genocide led to the deaths of up to one million people in Rwanda in the space of about a hundred days between April and July. Refugees poured across the borders to Zaire, Tanzania, Burundi and Uganda. The camps became full to overflowing. Children without parents were left with nowhere to go, nothing to eat and no-one to love or comfort them in an atmosphere of fear and utter despair. It was warm enough in the day time for the youngsters, but the nights in the rainy season towards the end of the year were bitterly cold and damp in their tented temporary homes. We discovered that aid workers were crying out for warm clothing, so we appealed to our viewers to knit jumpers and we hoped for around 25,000 by Christmas. Schools, societies, clubs and individuals laid into the challenge and, astonishingly, the total received rose by tens of thousands week after week. The final figure reached about a quarter of a million. An aid nurse, Ailsa Denney, told us on the programme that the children's eyes positively lit up when they saw the mass of bright colours, knitted in homes across Britain, and realised there would be no more shivering through the night. Will Hanrahan visited the camps twice and broadcast live from Ndosho near Goma in Zaire, just six days before Christmas. He took the latest consignment of jumpers with him and the kids dived on them. Bearing in mind the awfulness of the situation, it still made a happy scene as Will chatted to aid workers, held babies and joined in with the children's singing at the end of a memorable outside broadcast of which producer Claire Boulter and editor Tessa Finch could feel rightly proud.

The kidnapping of a young Birmingham estate agent captured the nation's attention in January 1992. Stephanie Slater had been showing a potential buyer round a house - we later learned that she was raped and kept in a wheelie-bin for eight days. Her captor released her outside her parents' home on receipt of a ransom of £145,000 and we all took Stephanie to our hearts after hearing about her courage in the face of such a frightening ordeal. Detectives released as much information as they could via BBC's Crimewatch UK programme. Crucially, it included his voice, taped from ransom demands he made to Stephanie's office. It was recognised by Michael Sams' ex-wife Susan and she phoned the police. In the end, Sams was convicted of Stephanie's kidnap, the murder of Julie Dart from Leeds and threatening to firebomb a store and derail a passenger train. He received two life sentences.

Teena Sams, who was married to Michael at the time of the offences, was one of our first guests in the new series of Anne and Nick in October 1993. From the beginning of the interview, Teena was beside herself with grief and guilt. She told us she had no idea what had been going on.

"There was nothing strange about his behaviour whatsoever. Every morning he got up, went to work, came home at a certain time every day. We had dinner together and then we sat and watched television."

I asked if it was true he called her in during Crimewatch. "Yes, at that present time, he was lying full length on the settee. I was making a cup of tea in the kitchen. He called me and said it's on. I went into the living room. I sat on a chair by the side of him. A picture came on about this Crimewatch and, the way he was talking and recording, no way did I put two and two together."

But how on earth did she not recognise his voice? That is what amazed people.

"How can I explain it? My husband's only got one leg. There are only certain things that people can do with one leg. Fair enough, I did say 'we live by a railway line, we live in a cottage, you've got a red Metro. Thank the Lord you have a tin leg.'

Anne: "Because you were absolutely sure that would have been recognised by anyone?"

Teena: "Yes, there's no way that he can disguise his leg."

She admitted she had been very hurt when she realised that he had kidnapped Stephanie and murdered Julie Dart. She felt betrayed.

In an appeal to her husband's victims and their families for forgiveness she added, "I swear to the Lord I did not know."

During our interview, I told Teena that Julie Dart's mother, Lynne, had phoned the studios in a highly emotional state to say she found it hard to believe her. As the interview continued, that was superseded by a further message from Lynne Dart, who said she had changed her mind and did now believe her. Meanwhile, Teena confirmed some truly bizarre details. For instance, her husband had washed and ironed Stephanie's clothes while she was held as a prisoner. The couple had been planning to adopt and were some way down the line with Social Services. "Unfortunately, during this time, my husband was doing wrong."

The staggering denouement to all this came half an hour later, when Stephanie Slater herself turned up at Pebble Mill and joined us on the sofa to sit alongside Teena Sams. She was incredibly strong and supportive of Teena. It was just so ironic to have the victim comforting the wife of the perpetrator. It seemed all the wrong way round. Teena clutched Stephanie's hand throughout and appeared on the verge of hyperventilating. Stephanie felt she and Teena were both victims and wanted to reassure her. "We will both go on suffering for a long time," she said.

Talking about Sams himself, she told us, "He was just plain evil." Her description of the fear she experienced was graphic. "That first night in the box I was told there were electrodes down one side and boulders above to fall down and crush me if I moved. I was chained with my hands above my head. I was very cold. It was freezing in there. I thought this is it. I have died."

After all that she had been through, she told us she had changed her perspective of life. "Trivialities don't interest me any more. I am alive. I don't worry about the cost of bread. I am grateful to be alive. After being that close to death you really see things in a different light. You just live for today." She added, "He should be kept where he is until he rots. Thank God the world is protected from him now."

As for Teena, she could hardly speak throughout the time Stephanie was with us, but she did manage to thank Lynne Dart and Stephanie for believing her and said, "This is the best day of my life. We have been through hell. Now I have peace of mind."

It was an astonishing morning and an impressive way to start a new series. Stephanie's calm and rational thinking, with no hint of the turmoil she must have been through, was quite staggering. She expressed herself with such eloquence. It has been suggested that Sams fell in love with her and that is what saved her life. Whatever, she was a remarkable young lady. I believed that Teena was totally unaware of her husband's activities, as I am sure everyone did, but I dread to think what sort of mental torture she went through in the ensuing years. As she said on the day to us, "If only I knew, I could have helped. But I didn't know anything."

People often ask what was my favourite interview and I have no difficulty in giving the answer. There are a few contenders. As I said earlier, Eric Morecambe was special and so too was the late country singer John Denver. His description of how he came to write his most famous hit, Annie's Song, was so beautifully vivid and evocative. One morning on breakfast television, he explained how he was way up on the ski slopes in the mountains of Colorado, well above the tree line, the sky a vibrant blue. With the distant swish swish of the skiers below, he said the beauty of it all "just filled up my senses." He felt inspired, raced down the slopes, hurried home and wrote Annie's Song for his wife within forty minutes. It was a remarkably descriptive couple of minutes and I remember telling

John what an exhilarating interlude it had been, listening to his spellbinding account of the making of a classic. He was a charismatic guest and I was deeply saddened when he died in a light aircraft crash in October 1997, at the age of 53.

So John Denver ranks high, but my clear winner is the morning we interviewed the former hostage, John McCarthy, on Good Morning with Anne and Nick. John, a television news producer, disappeared from view in April 1986, when he was kidnapped on the way to the airport in Beirut. We knew nothing of his welfare or whereabouts for more than five long years, but the brief film footage of him relaxing in the Lebanon sunshine became a familiar sight on our television screens. His girlfriend, Jill Morrell, strove heroically to keep his name in the public eye, so news of his release in August 1991 truly cheered the nation. It was announced to the crowd during the Test Match at the Oval, commuters were told on the tannoy on the London Underground and church bells pealed across the country. I can still recall where I was when I first heard about it...on the beach in Saundersfoot in South Wales with the family. I watched him return to RAF Lyneham in Wiltshire via a rather shaky outside broadcast on ITN. One of their less successful efforts, but nothing could dampen the impact of the moment John McCarthy appeared in the doorway of the aircraft, showing the world he was home at last. He had been in captivity for 1,943 days, been held in thirteen different locations and been chained to a radiator or wall bracket throughout. An unspeakable ordeal.

Jill and John joined us at Pebble Mill in April 1993 and I repeat it was the most moving, powerful interview I have ever had the privilege to do. They were an utterly charismatic couple with a compelling story to tell. He paid tribute to her unstinting loyalty and persistence in keeping his name to the forefront as she and the specially-formed Friends of John McCarthy group did everything in their power to hasten his release. He told us how desperate he felt after being told his mother had been dead for a year. The news came via two American hostages, Terry Anderson and Tom Sutherland, who had had a radio for some time. Inevitably, she had been one of his fantasy family and friends in his mind back home that sustained him during those dreadful times. "I had been living with her and coming home to her for a year when, in fact, she was dead, "he told us.

His particularly close friend during captivity was the Irishman Brian Keenan. Their sense of humour had played an important part in keeping them going. He also described the dramatic moment when another hostage was moved into the room next door to theirs. The new prisoner tapped on the wall using one tap for the letter A, two for B and so on. It was a very laborious process to work out in the end that their new neighbour was, in fact, Terry Waite.

The usual duration of an interview on Good Morning with Anne and Nick was four minutes. We spoke to Jill and John in two parts, six minutes and twelve, indicative of just how spellbinding it was. The company that handled our telephones estimated that we would normally have around six thousand people a minute – yes, a minute – trying to get through to the show at peak times. When John and Jill were on, the phones became virtually silent. When the talking stopped, the lines went crazy. And the viewers confirmed that John's release was indeed one of those 'I knew where I was' moments.

One woman said she heard the news on the World Service in Denmark and cried with joy. Another picked it up in Tibet. A caller from Leeds said she was giving birth to baby daughter Joanne at the very moment the announcement was made. A woman called Lilly was making cakes at the time and forgot all about them. They were burned to a cinder. Another viewer said her new grandson had been named Luke John McCarthy Mynard in John's honour. And my favourite: a pilot announced John's release to his passengers 35,000 feet up and the aircraft positively shook with their cheering. It was a time of national euphoria and we felt the same on that memorable day Jill and John met Anne and Nick.

A lot of callers wanted to know if they would marry and both were understandably coy. John said, "We have already had a very happy ending. I have come home. We are both lucky we get on so well and we are very happy with the way things are going at the moment. Like any couple, we want to make sure it is the right moment to make a decision, particularly about having a family, that we are ready to look after each other and any children."

The last time I saw John, we were playing in a charity cricket match together in Luton. It was a lovely, sunny day full of families and fun, a typical English scene, the sort he once must have feared he would never see again. In the end, as most people know, Jill and John went their separate ways and I sincerely hope they are both happy and fulfilled with their lives today. Goodness, they deserve it.

Chapter Thirteen

LOUNGING IN LEATHER

Looking back on my infrequent diary entries from the Anne and Nick years, I am struck by how often I felt the stress of it all. On the very first day of the 93-94 series, I wrote, "Stomach churning….why do it?" A week or so later, I am saying, "Horrendous day, felt desperately wound up before going on air and things never got better!" We also felt frustrated about press coverage which always seemed to imply we were behind ITV's This Morning in the ratings and that was often not the case. They had an aggressive press and publicity machine and we realised they were worried about us because so many stories kept appearing in the papers doing us down. Fleet Street twigged it to a certain extent, because we occasionally got calls from their showbiz people warning us they had been on again with another story that was patently untrue. "You'll never guess what they are saying this time," was the sort of opening line we would get from the tabloids. Here's another line from my diary in November 1993, "Another ridiculous story floated from Granada. Star trying to stand it up. Alan Yentob (Controller BBC1) apparently to have crisis meeting about us with threat to take us off air. They must be panicking!" This was a mere fifteen shows into our second series and we went to produce another 435! Even another programme on the BBC had a dig. A Sunday afternoon show called Biteback ripped into us and at the end presenter Sue Lawley, rather sniffily, erected a huge question mark over our future. Coming from a fellow presenter on the same channel, it was nauseating and Alan Yentob was absolutely furious.

I also notice in the diary how often editor Mike Hollingsworth pulled us up about things. After one programme, I wrote, "Mike not happy. Feels we're not enjoying it and look tired. Don't agree, though it is one hell of a strain." Another time, I put down, "Mike furious with us". It was all fairly volatile and I started having aromatherapy "because of this near permanent state of stress and stomach pain." This entry in December summed up all our feelings. "Appalling press coverage today implying our ratings are being stuffed by Richard and Judy. What bollocks! Why don't people realise that we climb all morning from a near two million deficit to be equal or ahead by the end. A phenomenal achievement."

That apart, the show was a joy to present and I would repeat what I said earlier that overall it was the happiest time of my working life. Stress or no stress, relentless or not. It was all those contrasts that made it for me. We had some terrific messages from viewers, many of them really funny, and we read loads of them out on air, so that the theme would develop a life of its own. One day we asked for names appropriate to people's jobs or lifestyles. Our favourite came from Mr. Gotobed who lived in Little Snoring in Norfolk. Then there were the calls about the funny things children say. It was sparked off by Anne's son Ollie asking his grandfather if he had fought the Romans. The classic came from the mother of a four-year-old schoolgirl who was constantly being asked in the playground to lift up her skirt so the boys could see her knickers. "I've foxed them now," the little girl told her family. "I've taken them off and put them in my lunchbox."

Our own children have delighted us with their remarks over the years. Tim was having tea with a few fellow four-year-olds when something fell off the table. "Why do things keep falling down?" asked one youngster. "It's because of a thing called gravity," Jill replied. Tim: "Have you got gravity at your house, Sean?"

Number three boy, Chris, delivered the best of all, though. Besides once asking the deeply philosophical question at the age of six, "Dad, why do we have life?" he also wondered one Bank Holiday why we were not doing a show. "Couldn't you think of anything?" he asked. The real beauty, though, came up when brother Andy came home after his first few weeks away at boarding school. With a mixture of relief to be back and anxiety over the rigours of boarding, Andy shed a tear or two as he entered the kitchen. "He's crying because he's happy and sad at the same time," Jill told the other three children. Chris: "Does that mean there'll be a rainbow?" Sheer magic. Talk about lateral thinking!

The Channel Tunnel officially opened on Friday May 6th 1994 and we celebrated with a live show from the market square in Boulogne. "We are no longer an island," proclaimed Anne and, in recognition of such an historic occasion, it poured with rain for much of the morning. Umbrellas were the order of the day, as Anne and I shivered for two hours, our scripts became smudged and we endured loads of technical problems. Anne even took to wearing gloves for the last hour. Guests such as the recently-voted most famous Frenchman Sacha Distel, who has now sadly left us, Vicky Michelle and Arthur Bostrom (both from the series 'Allo 'Allo!) helped carry the day. One time, as the cameras cut back to us, Sacha was helpfully wiping water from my forehead. "You have raindrops falling on your head," he intoned. It was a challenging operation with reporters bringing us news from both ends of the new tunnel, Jeni Barnet on the beach looking vainly in the gloom for the white cliffs across the other side, chef Glyn Christian talking recipes and weatherman Ian McCaskill playing with seaweed. "It's back to basics," he said. Showbiz reporter Tania Bryer and consumer expert Will Hanrahan both joined us in the square before Anne and I flew home later, somewhat comatose and slightly entwined, in the back of a six-seater aircraft.

Later that same year, we presented Guten Morgen with Anne and Nick from Germany to mark the fifth anniversary of the coming down of the Berlin wall. Two poignant events stand out for me from that memorable programme. The actor Andrew Sachs, best known as Manuel from Fawlty Towers, talked to us about his Berlin background. He was born there and spent the first eight or so years of his life in the city. He pointed out that the day was also another important anniversary, albeit a grim one. It was exactly fifty six years ago that Germans looted seven thousand shops and burned down hundreds of synagogues in an organised campaign of terror and, indeed, slaughter against the Jews. It became known infamously as Kristallnacht, a gruesome prelude to the horrors to come in World War Two. Equally chilling to hear was Andrew's memory of the night the family went for a meal at a restaurant after a trip to the circus. The police came in, checked his Jewish father's papers and led him away. The officer said to young Andrew's mother, "You won't see your husband again."

Happily, they did see him again and the family fled to England and safety. Although he was once called a 'dirty, German, Jewish pig', Andrew talked gratefully of the British reputation for taking in refugees. "It's wonderful and I owe my life to it."

The programme carried the theme of reunion and none was more touching than that of a Derbyshire woman who had befriended a German teenage prisoner-of-war in the forties. He was kept in a camp on the site of what is now Derbyshire County Cricket Club. He met a young Hazel Browne, but they lost touch after the war when he returned to East Germany. Hazel joined us in Berlin with husband Peter and, in front of the cameras, she saw Werner Kupper for the first time in 47 years. Their embrace was long, tearful and extremely moving.

I was particularly proud of that show, produced by Nick Thorogood, because it was packed with some remarkably interesting journalism, as a lot of our shows were. In fact, we were sometimes criticised for having too much heavy stuff on Anne and Nick, compared with the lighter fare on the other side. I would have thought the contrast was a good thing, but, that apart, we had scores of lighter moments too and some terrific laughs.

I loved my afternoon on a bed at the Savoy with Cher. She had been a guest in the studio previously and we had struck up a good relationship, so to coincide with the release of her new single about Elvis, we arranged a special visit to her hotel room in London. Pandering to her raunchy image, I dressed up in leather head-to-toe and arrived by motor bike. We played her video with shots of me looking almost rugged, but not quite, cleverly interspersed amid the original action before I stole upstairs to Room 412. I knocked on the door. "Who is it?" she called. "A friend", I replied. She opened the door in a dazzlingly bright red wig, said, "Nick, I have plans for you" and wrenched me inside. It was a great chat. Referring to her new song, she talked about Elvis and how he had once phoned her. "He asked me to go and see him at Las Vegas for the weekend," she told me. "We talked for about fifteen minutes and I was kinda nervous. I didn't go. I didn't know if I was going to see him or going to SEE him!" We talked about plastic surgery and she neither confirmed nor denied anything, we bantered and laughed a lot.

Not quite so many laughs, though, when Michael Jackson's sister La Toya visited us in March 1994. She was so like a female version of Michael, it was positively spooky. We knew she was not keen to talk about him because he was facing charges of sexual abuse against a child, but she ended up giving us what amounted to a total condemnation of her brother by saying that she could not be a silent collaborator of his crimes against small innocent children. Inevitably, looking for journalistic balance, we challenged her because nothing had been proven. However, her response took my breath away. "I have seen the cheques made payable to the parents of these children," she said. "I don't know if these children were bought from the parents by Michael or not." Later, she and her husband Jack Gordon rather took the line that we had no care for abused children because of the way we were taking the interview. "My family pays an awful lot of money to get out of things," she told us. "I was there. I lived there. I know what goes on. Believe me, money talks." It all became fairly heated. It was hardly surprising that she only really wanted to talk about her music and her autobiography and we were planning to do that later in the programme. We were stunned half an hour on to be told by the producer that she had stormed out and there would be no more La Toya! A pity, but what there had been was compulsive stuff.

Not for the first time, we made headlines in November 1993, but this time on the BBC's main news bulletin at six o'clock.It was the day after the killers of little Jamie Bulger had been sentenced and we held a phone-in on why the brutal killing had happened and what should happen to the young perpetrators. Amazingly, one of the callers was Jamie's uncle James. He came on air and said he'd like to get the two young boys in a room and "I'd f***ing kill 'em." We were hardly ready for that! I said words to the effect that we'd have to leave it there and could not have talk like that on television though we understood how strong his feelings must have been at such a terrible time. I was at home that evening peeling potatoes, when up I popped as the lead item on the news. I was relieved to see that I handled it reasonably well, but a lot of viewers were disappointed that we cut James Bulger off so quickly.

Sixty two, sexy and proud was how we described our guest, Yvonne Vinall, one morning, when we revealed how she made a living as an artist's model, often in the nude. She told us she had been brought up from an early age to be proud of her body. "My mother told me that one day I would earn money from it," she said. "Sounds terrible in a way, but she was right." We invited three artists of different standing to produce their own impressions of Yvonne. A student, a professional and a talented amateur. She re-appeared from behind a screen with silk, scarlet drapes tastefully arranged around her otherwise naked body and settled down on a couch, to our left and behind us. As she chatted about her pose, the drapes separated and there for all to see was her complete manifesto. Anne and I had not realised until uproar broke out in our ears from all in the gallery including producer Claire Boulter and director Merrick Simmonds. "For God's sake, don't go in close," shouted Merrick. "Cut," yelled Claire. I looked round and there it was resplendent in the studio lights. I said, "Gosh, I wonder where you've put your microphone," before a voice in the gallery observed, "What a funny place to keep a hamster!" It was hard to keep a straight face.

Even in the early days of Anne and Nick, Anne undoubtedly found things a strain at times, with the workload of the show, being mum to her children and coping with the vagaries of her relationship with Mike. One day, she heard from her agent Jon Roseman that the BBC were sounding out replacements for her and, amazingly, had asked him about one of his other clients. Anne was deeply distressed, so much so that Mike decided she was in no fit state to present the programme. She left the building two minutes before we went on air! There was also the growing turmoil about Mike's future.

He had a habit of upsetting top brass with some of his more pioneering ideas. In 1994, we presented one show live from Harrods to mark the opening of their January sales with the actor Richard Gere. Inevitably, Harrods got a few mentions during the morning and it looked to the cynical like one big plug for the store. A couple of months later, I was presenting the show alone when notorious ex-gangster Frankie Fraser came on. He had spent forty years of his life behind bars and been described as the most violent man in Britain.

His girlfriend Marilyn Wisbey was with him, the daughter of a Great Train Robber. Fraser said he wished he had been part of the robbery, but he was on the run at the time and they were worried he was too high profile and too violent. It was hard not to be rude to someone with such an appalling reputation, but what was really difficult came later in the show. The best known of the Great Train Robbers, Ronnie Biggs, was facing possible extradition from Brazil and, with hardly any warning, I was told he was on the line from Rio de Janeiro to talk to me. BBC guidelines actually advise against any programme talking to a criminal on the run from British law, although that was not particularly in my mind at the time. While I was handling that, I became aware of Frankie Fraser sliding quietly back onto the sofa next to me. I was then told via talkback to get them to talk to each other. "Hi Frankie!" "Hi Ronnie, how are you doing!" type of stuff, with Fraser describing Biggs as a "smashing fella" and Biggs returning the compliment, saying Fraser was a "nice guy". It was all fairly distasteful to ordinary law-abiding folk and I hope I made that clear at the time.

Mike Hollingsworth really wanted to run the whole of the morning output, not just our show, and he certainly had the flair to make anything worth watching. But he sure knew how to upset people and, in the end, after a number of clashes, he resigned. Following much speculation, Tessa Finch was announced as his successor. She was already on board as an assistant producer, but her meteoric promotion was a shock to everyone. Alan Yentob said she had given the best interview he had ever heard. In my diary, I say, "Mike devastated and Anne hit the roof." Ironically, Mike had persuaded Tessa to apply in the first place, but the reality obviously did not please him at all. He still wanted to continue himself and was clearly hurt that the BBC had accepted his resignation. As for myself, I wrote in the diary, "I have huge doubts over her acute lack of experience, but what can you do if she's been offered the job and said yes? Anne lays into Rod Natkiel and David Wain (two senior managers at Pebble Mill), then goes to Yentob in London who seems shocked at a number of things. The pot continues to bubble. The fat lady remains in her dressing room."

In fact, we produced some memorable programmes under Tessa, as I have already described, but she and Anne never really saw eye to eye. Anne once started a blazing row with her, including the odd four letter word, on the studio floor to the astonishment of some nearby guests. She made a number of trips to London to air her grievances with Alan Yentob. He was apparently not too impressed with her behaviour and, within minutes of her departure, would be on the phone to his management colleagues at Pebble Mill in disparaging mode. The climate hardly augured well for the show's long-term future.

Chapter Fourteen

SAY IT WITH FLOWERS

Good Morning with Anne and Nick came to an end after six hundred programmes in May 1996. Virtually all the current team of the time joined in that day; Doctor Mark Porter, gardening expert Professor Stefan Buczacki, fashion reporter Ollie Picton-Jones, drinks doyen Oz Clarke, showbiz correspondent Catrina Skepper, Ainsley Harriott and Will Hanrahan. The cast of 'Allo, 'Allo!, who were about to start a British tour, also took part and helped us get through what turned out to be a fairly tough day. We were deluged with messages from viewers who were sad to see the show coming off and even received a telegram from Radio Five Live, saying they were all watching in the newsroom and were 'heartbroken' at our demise. It was undoubtedly a popular show and people still come up to me several times a week, saying how much they miss it. I know that BBC daytime has had some successes in the morning since, but none, in my opinion, have created the identity or branding of the schedules headlined by Kilroy, Anne and Nick, then Pebble Mill with Alan Titchmarsh and Judy Spiers. Ask anyone in the street now what they expect to see on BBC in the morning and I think many would struggle to give you a definitive answer. That is not to decry the programmes that are on at the moment….it is just that they lack the stamp of the first half of the nineties.

Various reasons were given for taking us off. The ratings had fallen a little, but that was inevitable once the BBC had made it clear earlier in the year that we were finishing and implicitly withdrew its support. Over the four years, figures had stood up well. We were told we were too similar to This Morning on the other side. I can understand that to some extent, but Anne and I were very different personalities from Richard and Judy and we directed ourselves far more to hard new stories. I strongly believe that people want topical, live magazine programmes at that time of the day....it is hardly surprising that they are similar, in the same way as the Daily Mail or Daily Express could be described as similar. People make their choice with that knowledge, or have a look at both. No, I am firmly of the opinion that we were getting too many headlines, we were quite expensive at about £60,000 a show and someone somewhere at the top had taken against us. In other words, politics.

I was sad, Anne was furious, as she showed the moment we came off air. The head of broadcasting, Nigel Chapman, addressed all the team in the conservatory part of our studio at Pebble Mill. Alongside him were the editor, Tessa Finch, and her deputy, Katie Wright. He read out a faxed message from Alan Yentob; "A big thanks for all the hard work, professionalism and dedication over the past four years" and then presented us with some flowers. Anne's sumptuous bouquet of lilies and chrysanthemums apparently cost £75, but she was not to be swayed. She stormed up to Nigel, threw the flowers onto the ground and said: "Unfortunately I cannot accept these because of the hypocrisy of the BBC. The number of times I have been up and down that motorway to see Alan Yentob to discuss the programme." In other words, she thought he was sympathetic to her and the programme, but obviously that was not the case. She felt badly let down, as I did too. It has to be remembered also that it was acutely disappointing for all the staff on the programme and many of them were wondering where their futures lay. I am happy to say that most of them spread out to all parts of the television world, some of them with singular success. Most notable in front of the camera has been Ainsley Harriott, while Tessa has continued to rise up the management structure, currently heading network broadcasting in the Midlands.

On that final morning in May 1996, I led Anne away to our small office, where we had a drink, said goodbye to our colleagues and drove away. Jill had booked us a weekend in one of our favourite haunts, Guernsey, so we headed south to Gatwick that evening, ready to fly out the next morning. As we waited in the departure lounge, it became increasingly obvious that Anne's outburst was plastered all over the newspapers. With quizzical looks, our fellow passengers stared constantly in our direction.

So came to an end my happy partnership with Anne Diamond. She has had some terrible things written about her over the years and a report about her, put together after a survey among Good Morning viewers, was particularly damning. They used words and phrases such as distant, snotty, stuck-up, patronising, condescending and too rigid with her body language. One particular quote knocked us both; "Look at her. Look at her silly face. Like a dummy. Dummies the pair of them." All Booker Prize stuff and described by a BBC executive as "dynamite."

On the other hand, there were some supporters too. Viewers recognised her strong journalistic skills, her superb interviewing technique and the way she talked to camera. It is no surprise that I am very much in the supporters' camp. Anne is an excellent presenter, with something that is too often taken for granted....the ability to talk naturally to a lump of metal with a genuine care and understanding for your subject. She felt, and feels, passionately about the work she does, but she does not suffer fools gladly and this has rubbed many people up the wrong way over the years, right back to her early days. She has laid into colleagues without thinking and I have seen a programme editor reduced to tears after one of her verbal assaults. I could never approve of that. She was always fiercely ambitious, too transparently so, and that has never been as acceptable in a woman as it seems to be for a man. She often tended to be preoccupied and unaware sometimes of what was going on around her. More than once, we would be greeted by a couple of cameramen in the corridor and she would totally ignore them. She simply had not noticed because she was cocooned in her own little world at the time. Trouble is, it just seemed bloody rude. I must say, I thought she was a bit full of herself when I first had dealings with her at ATV back in 1979, but, once we were thrust together in a working partnership, we got on really well and both knew we had a special relationship on and off-screen. We were described in the newspapers as going together like bacon and eggs, and we probably spent more time in each other's company than we did with our respective spouses. People are constantly asking me these days how she is and if we keep in touch and I am always impressed by how genuinely concerned they are for her. Whatever

138

those surveys implied, I believe most members of the public have a strong regard for Anne, an affection for her and sympathy for what she has been through, with her battle against her weight, her troubled marriage and, of course, the tragedy of baby Sebastian. I have seen her at high points and lows, we have shared secrets we would never share with anyone else, we know all each other's respective skeletons and we have a trust that neither of us will ever betray. It may be that some of the things she said and did seriously upset the top brass at the BBC. Director General John Birt was apparently incandescent after she signed up to present a lucrative advertising campaign with ITV, when she was hosting Good Morning. News journalists do not do adverts. It is claimed that he wanted her off BBC screens immediately, but later relented. It may be that some producers and directors vowed never to work with her again, if they could avoid it, because of her sharp tongue. These negative factors may have hastened the demise of Anne and Nick, but, equally, you will find former colleagues who thoroughly enjoyed working alongside her. They, of course, do not make the headlines, but those who loved her, really loved her. I count myself lucky to have worked so closely with her for so long. People were often intrigued by our relationship. Just how close did we get? Well, we were intrigued too! There was a huge frisson between us and we were very tactile, but no affair. I will leave it at that.

She put up with a lot from me with my sometimes painful sense of humour. I remember Mike telling me to cut back on the gags once because they were a bit too near the mark. She was actually quite chaste, in a way, with her upright family background and Roman Catholic upbringing. She had once completed a recipe session in the kitchen when she handed back to me and I remarked that Anne had always wanted to get her hands on Ainsley's goujons. We were swamped with complaints and she did look a little shocked herself. Another time, they had a huge salmon in the cooking area and, as I joined them, I commented on the terrible stink. "I just hope the fish will get used to it", I said. Anne had a voracious appetite for Ainsley's tasty offerings. Occasionally he would ferret around beneath the cooker for one he had made earlier and find it had been devoured earlier! We once had a famously gay guest talking to us in the kitchen and I suggested to Anne I was going to ask him if he would like to sit next to the mincer so that he would feel at home. If looks could kill! I told her one morning that our gardening wizard Stefan Buczacki had been taken to hospital with violent stomach pains, after accidentally swallowing a bag of daffodil bulbs. The doctor had warned he would have to stay in for a while, but he should be out in the spring. Agony Aunt Claire Rayner was once helping a troubled forty-year-old man on our phone-in. Because of problems down below, he was facing a circumcision operation the following week. I had to break in. "George, we've run out of time, so I will have to cut you off." How I wish I had never said that. Our diet expert once told a woman, worried about her weight, that she was obese. She was not too happy and demanded a second opinion. "OK, you're ugly as well." he said.

Anne got a bit of a shock one day when she nipped to the loo while we were showing a filmed report. Our next item was to feature sexy underwear for men and we had a hunky, dance troupe, similar to the Chippendales, lined up to model them. As Anne walked behind the scenes, she found the men getting ready. Standing to attention, in fact. They were passing round a bottle of baby oil and applying it to relevant areas of their anatomies to make sure their credentials would look their best and be up for the job!

The studio crew on Anne and Nick were a terrific bunch, particularly cameraman Howard Dartnall. He is the sort of guy who will frequently greet you with the old favourite: "Hiya, nice to see you back in men's clothing!" The sort of guy that, if he was on fire, you would dial 998! He became a great friend and his one-liners were legendary. I bumped into him the other day and he had been working on a gardening programme. "That Charlie Dimmock," he said. "She's certainly got her knockers, but I think she's very good!" He told me he sprayed brandy onto his lawn so that the grass would come up half-cut. One week when Anne was off ill, we kept inventing new reasons for her absence. The first day we said it was a back problem...she could not lift it off the bed. Then we decided she had broken something...a fingernail. The final one, I remember, was disc trouble. Her CD player had packed up. He gave me a load of brilliant groaners day after day and so did another mate, John Payne, who used to write jokes for Jasper

Carrott, amongst others. In fact, Jasper put me onto him and I still frequently talk to John for a line or two, whether for Midlands Today or an after-dinner speech. My favourite groaner from John is about the farmer who gives whisky to his hens. Now they are laying Scotch eggs!

During the run of Anne and Nick, I was deeply saddened to lose two people who had played an important part in my life. Firstly, Billy Wright, the man who gave me my first real chance in television and I thank him for that. A sporting hero if ever there was one, Billy gave outstanding service to Wolves and England over an impeccable 21 year career, before becoming a TV executive. He died of cancer in 1994 and the whole of Wolverhampton seemed to be lining the streets in tribute on the day of his funeral. Another colleague at ATV, later my agent, Peter Plant, suffered terribly with bone cancer before dying in the early hours of Christmas Day 1996. Jill and I visited him late on Christmas Eve, when he was clearly close to the end, but it was a bitter blow when his wife Maureen called with the sad news on Christmas morning. He had been a wonderful friend and supporter, an absolute gentleman, but a fearsome negotiator on behalf of his clients. I was lucky enough to be taken on by KnightAyton Management afterwards, who represent a host of big name news broadcasters. Sue Knight and Sue Ayton have done me proud and become loyal friends.

As Good Morning with Anne and Nick closed, a number of new opportunities opened up, albeit short term. Almost immediately, Jill and I plus our two youngest, Chris and Jenny, went on a Mediterranean cruise at the invitation of my cousin Chris Dean. Chris is the son of my mother's sister, Yvonne, and is a hugely talented musician. Once lead trombonist in the British Army, he moved into the freelance world and made a formidable name for himself around the big band circuit. After working with the renowned band leader Syd Lawrence, he bought the business off Syd and the Syd Lawrence band is now, in fact, the Chris Dean band, playing some wonderful stuff, particularly Glenn Miller, around the country. I have been privileged occasionally to join them all on stage and say a few words. They are absolutely superb. Chris was handling entertainment for a cruise line at the time and asked me to give a number of talks during our fourteen day trip around the Med. It was a fantastic experience.

I also presented a series of football chat shows for Tyne Tees Television in Newcastle. It was meant to be a mix between light entertainment and football and, again, it was terrific fun. Regular panellists included Tyneside heroes Bobby Moncur and John Burridge, but we were also joined, amongst many others, by Malcolm Macdonald and even the absolute legend, Len Shackleton. He used to delight my father's generation with his magic on the field. He confirmed that once, before a massive crowd at Arsenal, he stopped running, put his foot on the ball, called the ref over, asked for a comb and proceeded to arrange his hair …all during normal play. Another time, apparently, he just sat on the ball while the other twenty one players waited for his next outrageous move. Everyone seems to be football daft in the north east. I had only been in my hotel five minutes on my first visit when a waitress came up and asked me totally out-of-the-blue, "What do you think of Kenny Dalglish?" There would be families of four or five, who would take it in turns to use the two family season tickets. Some lovely stories emerged on the show. Bobby Moncur recalled how many of the Newcastle team he captained were smokers. He told me they would come in at half-time and manager Joe Harvey would be waiting with six cigarettes already lit for the players as they returned to the dressing room. How times and attitudes have changed! During one show, there was talk of the terrible state of some pitches, all mud and no grass. One wag suggested they took a tip from Bobby Charlton and grew the grass really long down one touchline, then combed it across to the other side.

I also hosted a topical news quiz in London for Carlton Television, where one of my regular panellists was someone I had never heard of before, Graham Norton. He was brilliantly funny and it is no surprise to me that he has gone on to become so successful. He was not quite so outrageous then, though. It was an early evening show and it went so well, Carlton wanted to put it out later. However, they felt a prime time slot would demand a bigger budget and the company felt they could not afford it. A real disappointment, because it was a terrific show, which was down to the high quality of guests and the brilliant writing of the producer, Kate Copstick. She taught me a lot about how to deliver a gag and that has helped me considerably since, particularly with after-dinner speaking. Talking about game shows, I enjoyed my guest spot on the sports satirical quiz, They Think It's All Over. Some weeks afterwards, a little old lady said she had seen me on 'that funny sports questions programme'. I said, "They Think It's All Over." "I'm sorry to hear that," she replied.

Cilla Black's Surprise Surprise programme roped me in to take a woman who loved huskies across to the United States to run them in the snow of the Rocky Mountains. What an exhilarating experience that was! My journey took me through places such as Lookout Mountain, Muddy Creek, Rabbits Ears Pass, via Buffalo Bill's grave to Steamboat Springs. The lady concerned, an ex-patriate Dutchwoman, called Ali Koops, drove a ten-strong team from her sledge, while I scooted about on a snowmobile in totally breathtaking scenery, so remote, so white, so quiet. On the way back to Denver Airport after negotiating blizzards and avalanches, we stopped for a breather at the Buffalo Bar in Idaho Springs. The waitress came up to me and said, "Hi, Nick, I recognise you from television. I once served you and your family when I was living in Tenby in South Wales." Small world!

I started a documentary series around about this time with Meridian Television on the history of the English Channel. It was fascinating to do, albeit on a shoestring. I travelled round the south coast, taking an informal look at the places and events that had shaped our history from the times before there was any water in the Channel right up to the Second World War. I am as proud of that series as anything I have ever presented on television. I later went back to Meridian for a series of consumer shows, called Streetwise. All enjoyable work, average pay, but always short-term and that was a problem. Without real security, Jill and I could never be sure where the next contract was coming from, so paying the mortgage became a worry. We also still had four children at private schools. It was a tough decision because we loved it where we were in Edgbaston in Birmingham, but, with heavy heart, we decided we would have to sell our house to move to a less expensive area and that we did in the summer of 1997.

By that time, I had been invited to take over as presenter for the BBC's regional news programme, Midlands Today. That turned out to be an extremely happy move. At the time of writing I am heading for the end of my seventh year in the job, the longest I have stayed anywhere. My main partners have been Sue Beardsmore and Suzanne Virdee, both of whom I knew fairly well before working with them in the studio. Sue is quite a bit taller than I am, so for certain publicity photos, I had to stand on a box! On the first night, we had an outside broadcast from the impressive Council House in the centre of Birmingham. As the camera panned around the magnificent banqueting hall, I ad-libbed, "This is where the Lord Mayor holds his balls and dances."

Sue, my co-presenter for the early days with the programme, has moved on to working behind the scenes now, after twenty years presenting various programmes for BBC Midlands. She and Kay Alexander, another long-time presenter in the region, are two of the best-known and most popular faces in the region. Traditionally, the ITV regional audience figures have been ahead of the BBC's, but I am delighted to say that the BBC dominates the ratings these days, sometimes by as much as three to one. My current on-screen partner Suzanne is terrific to work with and a close friend. The same goes for our weather presenter, Shefali Oza, a law graduate who has become an icon in the Midlands. Besides the mix of serious news and light-hearted banter, I have been lucky enough to keep up my contacts with the showbiz figures I have come to know over the years and interviewed many of them in special features for the programme. They include Gene Pitney, Joan Collins, Chris de Burgh, Sir Cliff Richard, Jim Davidson, Michael Crawford, Englebert Humperdinck, Lenny Henry, Des O'Connor, Tommy Steele, Status Quo and many more. I am lucky enough to work with a cracking team, very hard working and seriously enthusiastic. Some of them were not born when I started in television and that can be quite sobering. And, yes, I did once hear the question, "Is it true Paul McCartney was in another group before Wings?" Alright then, I once heard about someone else who heard it.

Presenting Midlands Today gave me an opportunity for which I shall be forever grateful. It presented me with the chance to take my father back to the beaches of Dunkirk. It would be the first time he had been there since the horrors of the evacuation in World War Two sixty years ago. It would be an understatement to say it was a very special occasion, but Bertie Owen is a very special man.

Chapter Fifteen

BACK TO THE BEACHES

My father Bertie has influenced me in so many ways. As a much-loved headmaster in Berkhamsted for more than twenty years, he was renowned for treating colleagues, parents and boys with equal respect, exceptionally sensitive to the feelings of others and always generous with his time. Nothing was ever too much trouble. He taught many of my closest friends and all, to a man, seem to have the utmost affection for him and indeed for my mother Esme, who supported him constantly and loyally in her dual role as music teacher and headmaster's wife. He is a gentleman and a gentle man and I dearly hope that some of his qualities have rubbed off on me. I could never hope to rival his achievements, though. He won a scholarship to Shrewsbury School, played for the first eleven football and cricket teams, edited the school magazine, won a hatful of prizes, became Head of School and landed a classics scholarship to Cambridge University. Those are just the headlines when he was still in his teens! He became a teacher, but that was put on hold very quickly at the onset of war in 1939.

That he survived those dreadful years and particularly the potential disaster of Dunkirk benefited thousands of schoolboys and, amazingly, some of his earlier pupils are now in their seventies and even eighties and in regular contact to this day. He always looked for the best in his youngsters, the silver lining in every cloud, and I cannot imagine that any mums and dads have ever put their most treasured possessions in the hands of a more conscientious guardian.

He imbued me with a passion for sport from my earliest years and that is something I am eternally grateful for. He took me to my first cricket Test Match in the summer of 1958 and my first professional football match in the autumn of that same year. Obviously, I was interested enough to want to go in the first place, but once I had sampled the atmosphere at the Oval as England took on New Zealand, my fate was sealed and a passion was born. Only a pity that we saw a mere three overs bowled, no runs scored and then incessant rain for the rest of the day. Just a few weeks later, Bertie took me down the road to the First Division match between Luton Town and Leeds United and the impact was even more dramatic. We drew one all and my burgeoning enthusiasm for Luton exploded into what has become a lifelong devotion. It has been inherited by my two oldest boys, Andy and Tim, but it is not unusual for all four children to travel to games with me, home or away. I tell people it has given me more than forty years of misery and there have definitely been a huge number of low points, but there have been some great moments too and I could not possibly imagine supporting any other team. I just cannot understand people who live in Plymouth or Hull and support Manchester United. I passionately believe in the concept of following your local side, either where you were born or grew up, or where you currently live. If we all just picked and chose according to results and glamour, we would only need Arsenal, Chelsea, Manchester United, Liverpool, perhaps one or two more, and we could' change every season depending on who won the latest title. As a Luton Town supporter, I have never been accused of being a glory-seeker!

There have been heady times, though. We reached the FA Cup Final in 1959 and I cried when we lost two one to Nottingham Forest. The following season saw the start of a staggering decline. In 1960, we were playing in the top division. By 1965, we were in Division Four, with a very real danger the next season of going out of the league. I remember travelling from Leeds University to a match at Hartlepool and I was the only Luton fan there. We lost 2-1. That same season, we were thumped 8-1 at Lincoln City, our very nadir, but a star of the future was emerging in Bruce Rioch. He top-scored the following season, played with exhilarating flair and we won the Fourth Division with a record number of points. Bruce went on to play for a host of top clubs and captained Scotland. Heroes such as Malcolm Macdonald came and went and, ultimately, Luton Town enjoyed their most successful spell in the eighties under David Pleat, John Moore and Ray

Harford. We got to a couple of FA Cup semi finals, finished in our highest-ever position in the old First Division (seventh) and reached Wembley in two consecutive seasons in the Littlewoods Cup. Memorably, we beat Arsenal 3-2 in a highly dramatic final in April 1988, when Brian Stein scored the winner with virtually the last kick of the match. Also playing in that match was centre-forward Mick Harford, who is now one of my closest friends. As I write, he and Brian are important members of the coaching set-up there, alongside manager Mike Newell, another former player at the club.

Our cup run of 1985 ended with semi-final defeat by Everton in a thriller at Villa Park after we had totally dominated the match, but it was marred by an appalling outbreak of violence from Millwall fans at our Kenilworth Road stadium in the round before. They invaded the pitch, ripped up seats, laid waste to parts of the ground and caused such mayhem that it dominated the headlines the following day. Manager David Pleat was sitting near me at the time and he was crestfallen, despite the fact we won one-nil. I remember trying to lift his spirits, but I did not expect to be interviewing him about it on the TVam sofa the next morning. In the end, Luton Town banned away fans and introduced a membership scheme for home supporters.

It is difficult to explain to a non-sports fan what it is like to have a passion for a team. You either get it or you do not. It eats so deeply into your system that it defies rational thinking. If you cannot get to a game, match-days are agony. Sometimes, I listen to commentary over the internet, but I often switch it off because I cannot bear the tension as the commentator's voice rises to a gut-wrenching crescendo, especially when the action is in our penalty box. If we are losing, I might leave the room to give us a chance of scoring. Then I go back in with dread a few minutes later. Before the wonders of the internet, I would frequently listen to BBC Three Counties Radio commentary but not in the house. Bearing in mind I live in Birmingham, only my car radio was strong enough to receive the signal. I could often be seen sitting outside the house in the front seat for ninety minutes to keep in touch. Basically, though, if I can make it to a match, I will be there. I am proud to say my boys are even more determined than I am and they travel the length and breadth these days to get to games. The weekend is totally coloured by Luton's result. If they lose, it takes me at least twenty four hours to come round and start thinking ahead, not back. I would rather not go out, if we have been beaten. Ridiculous, I know, but, as I said, you either get it or you don't. I was totally unprepared for a gesture by the club during the Anne and Nick days. It all boiled down to a plan first instigated by the club's Commercial Manager at the time, Kathy Leather. Anne Diamond heard about it, got our producers involved and one day, as I thought we were handing over to a live make-over item at a private house, I discovered the cameras were at Luton Town Football Club! There before my very eyes, they created a Nick Owen Lounge. I was so surprised and incredibly flattered. I often have a drink in there on match-days, but not every time. On one occasion, I was barred by an unsuspecting doorman. He had no idea who I was, but Health and Safety Regulations meant he was unable to let anyone in because it was packed to the rafters. As I walked away, another 'failed' customer asked the doorman if he knew who he had just turned away. He did not. "Well, his name's up there above your head, mate, in f***ing great capital letters!" I have had some stick about that ever since, but the poor steward had absolutely no option. Ironic, though, isn't it, banned from your own lounge!

Luton Town Football Club has been to the very depths again in recent times, but the resurrection has started and I hope we will soon be back in our rightful place in the First Division, at least, and in a brand new stadium right by the M1 motorway. The club encouraged the founding of a supporters' club in the mid-eighties and I was honoured to become its first President, a position I have held now for nearly twenty years. It has a reputation of an accessible and friendly set-up and I am fiercely proud of my long association with the club.

Although I was born and grew up on the Hertfordshire, Bedfordshire and Buckinghamshire border, I have a strong affinity with Derbyshire. My mother was brought up in Buxton and we still have family in the area. I still cherish very happy memories of holidays with my grandfather in that beautiful county and that is why my cricketing allegiance has always been with Derbyshire. Some combination, eh, Luton Town Football and Derbyshire County Cricket Club! Grandpa Wilf Burton was a sports nut too. He was a useful footballer with Buxton Town and attracted the attention of Manchester United. They wanted him to go for a trial, but his parents would not allow it because Manchester was so far away…all of twenty five miles! He had to travel a lot further shortly afterwards when he was called up for the First World War and spent four wretched years in the trenches in France, including Vimy Ridge. It always saddens me that I never knew my other three grandparents.

So I have followed Derbyshire County Cricket Club since the late fifties and they are now dragging themselves into the twenty-first century at what used to be a rickety old ground in Derby. The place has been transformed in recent years, with an excellent new pavilion and indoor school recently opened. The club has produced some fine cricketers over the years, including Cliff Gladwin, Les Jackson, Alan Ward, Mike Hendrick, Bob Taylor, Geoff Miller, Devon Malcolm, Kim Barnett, John Morris, Dominic Cork and a particular friend of mine, Chris Adams, all of whom have played for England. It is not the most glamorous of outfits, but as I implied earlier, once you have a club in your blood, there it stays. I have had a long association with Warwickshire too and count many of their players, past and present, as good friends too. Son Andy works at Edgbaston and has played for the county seconds, while his younger brother Tim went on a South Africa tour with the club's under-nineteens. You hardly ever meet an unpleasant person in cricket because the game's unique charm, in my opinion, only entices a certain kind of individual. It is utterly captivating, with its own special charisma, borne of the many subtleties denied to other sports. It takes a lot of getting to know, but it is certainly worth it. You may not get tens of thousands at day-to-day county matches, because ordinary working people cannot spare the time, but the interest in following the scores either through newspapers, the internet or text on television is immense. If I have a spare hour or two, I have no hesitation in racing to Derby, Edgbaston or Worcester for a quick visit to soak up the rich atmosphere and friendship that, for me, only cricket can provide. Just for good measure, I have a square of turf from Lord's growing in my back garden, kindly given to me by a cricket mad viewer of Midlands Today!

As a teenager, my father frequently used to cycle with his friends from Shrewsbury to Worcester to watch cricket. One time, they even biked it to Kent, the best part of two hundred miles, and toured the cricket festivals at Canterbury, Folkestone and Dover. He has particularly fond memories of seeing Don Bradman score a century before lunch for the visiting Australians. And people ask me where I get my passion from! I wonder how many would be prepared to ride so far nowadays on our congested, polluted and dangerous roads. That was in the comparatively carefree period of school and university, before he started work and then signed up for the army as our eastern horizon darkened with the imminent threat of Hitler and Nazi Germany.

He joined the Royal Army Service Corps and crossed the English Channel with the British Expeditionary Force early in 1940. He was at Lille in France when the Belgians surrendered to the advancing Germans and the British forces had to retreat. I grew up knowing he was at Dunkirk where the remarkable evacuation of 338,226 troops occurred under fearsome attack from the enemy, but Bertie had never talked about it. Until one dramatic Sunday lunchtime at our house fifty-five years after the event.

I cannot remember how the conversation turned to it, but all of a sudden he was talking about Dunkirk. He is not given to showing much visible emotion, but on that truly memorable day, in front of my mother, my wife and our four children, he wept. I can still see our faces around the table, as he unloaded those painful memories that he had suppressed for so long. It was harrowing and even little Jenny at six years old was open-mouthed. He told how he stood for at least 24 hours, either on the sand or in the water, under constant bombardment, looking out to sea, hoping that a rescue boat would come. He constantly witnessed people being killed or maimed. He even saw a Spitfire crash. Even so, he remembered some humorous interludes. "A man in my unit turned to me in a quiet moment between gunfire to say his missus wouldn't half be jealous, when she heard he'd been to the seaside before her that year!"

He was a second lieutenant in the Service Corps, which was a troop-carrying unit. He recalled the last moments before they headed for the beaches. "We had to move our vehicles to Dunkirk and leave them in a field to be blown up so that they would be no good to the Germans. As we were picking up the troops, you could see the Germans approaching in their tanks and armoured cars." Men poured onto the beaches in their thousands and the only way out was across the sea. "The place was in turmoil," he said. "Night never seemed to fall, because the constant flash of shells, bombs and gunfire meant it was always light."

Then came the escape. "The buzz went round in the early morning that a destroyer had come in. The ship was called the Sabre and I was among the lucky ones to get on board. I don't remember eating in all that time. I think I had lost my appetite, but I did have a couple of tots of rum when I got on board. We sailed in daylight and we were being constantly attacked from the air, so we helped form a chain to pass shells to the anti-aircraft guns."

The soldiers' spirit changed the course of history, enabling the British army to rise up again and ultimately, with allied help, crush the Nazis. Winston Churchill wrote: "In the midst of our defeat, glory came to the island people, united and unconquerable; and the tale of the Dunkirk beaches will shine in whatever records are preserved."

In 2000, my colleagues at BBC Midlands Today suggested I might like to take Bertie back to the beaches on the sixtieth anniversary of that pivotal moment in British history. I was delighted when he agreed and I cannot possibly put into words how proud I felt as he marched with ramrod back through the streets and square of Dunkirk alongside hundreds of fellow veterans, all carrying their individual memories. We found the field where he had dumped his truck sixty years ago and we stood on the sand where he had spent those terrifying hours that saw so many thousands of lives lost. In 1940, he was assaulted by the sounds of explosions, gunfire and the cries of the wounded...this time the laughter of happy holidaymakers. It was an astonishing contrast. I treasure the photographs from that day and the film we showed on the BBC. And, of course, if he had not come home, he would not have met the wonderful woman who became my mother, I would not have been born and the two of them would not have enjoyed their four marvellous grandchildren.

Chapter Sixteen

A STING IN THE TAIL

Do you remember how I suffered a gruesome wasp sting in a very delicate area of my groin when I was a little boy in short trousers? That cowardly attack left me with a tiny lump, but I had never taken much notice of it until the summer of 2003, when I sensed it was changing shape and texture. I told my doctor about it and he reckoned it should not be anything to worry about, but I should see a specialist just to make sure. The specialist, Francis Peart, was equally unperturbed, but he said he would remove it anyway and he did. The test results returned a week later and they shook us both. It was cancerous…. thanks to the chemical changes caused by that dastardly insect more than forty years earlier. Just briefly, your world stops on receiving such dreaded news. I really had not considered it. I would have to have a rather larger area removed and a skin graft taken from my hip to replace it. I rang Jill, Sue Knight, my agent and close friend in London, and my parents. I walked back to the hospital car park in a daze, although the specialist had assured me there was no cause for panic and the operation should be perfectly straightforward. My parents were fairly shaken, inevitably. After all, the 'c' word must be amongst the top five most fearful words in the language. I was due at work within the hour. When I arrived, I immediately told my editor and big mate, Chas Watkin, and producer Naomi Bishop. It was early December. I said I needed to come off the rota from Midlands Today almost immediately and I would not be back until the new year. I naturally confided in my co-presenter Suzanne Virdee and a couple of other close friends including Mick Harford and the incoming Luton Town chairman Bill Tomlins, but hardly anyone else at the BBC was told because I wanted the whole thing to remain as private as possible.

The operation took place later that week and, afterwards, I had to remain as still as possible to enable the skin graft to take. I had a stream of visitors, including Jasper Carrott and Bev Bevan, and they turned a few heads amongst the nursing staff, as you can imagine. Jill, of course, came once or twice a day, plus Suzanne, old friends Maurice Blisson and Andy Knowles, the children and my pal Tony Finch, a millionaire businessman, who loves football, cricket, wine, women and song as much as I do. The difference is that he travels the world following our Test side, while most of us are slaving away back here. He has watched England in Australia, Bangladesh, India, South Africa, Sri Lanka, the West Indies and Zimbabwe. He tends to ring me on the morning of the first day just to remind me he is there. This, of course, is not remotely irritating. However, he has yet to challenge my record of seeing three different county championship matches on the same day, which I did with son Chris on the first day of the 2003 season. We watched a couple of hours at Derby, took in the afternoon session at Trent Bridge, Nottingham and then scooted south for the last hour of the day at Worcester. Tony is one of the best known social figures on the cricketing circuit and he has served Midlands sportsmen superbly over the years. He has chaired around twenty benefits for footballers and cricketers and been at the forefront of raising at least £3 million in the process. I would describe him as a philanthropist, with the emphasis probably on the last syllable!

My operation was a complete success, the graft settled in well and a few weeks later I was given the provisional all-clear. Six months after that, Mr Peart again said things looked pretty good and discharged me. Many thanks to him and his team, but not the wasp. Incidentally, while both of us pointed the finger accusingly at that indiscriminate insect, Mr Peart mischievously suggested it could also have been wear and tear, in other words, overuse. Disgraceful! Happily, the problem never remotely appeared life-threatening, but an attack of acute pancreatitis five years earlier clearly was. I was woken in the night with dreadful stomach pains, but I put it down to a chicken pie I had eaten in the players' bar at Luton Town Football Club a few hours earlier. After I had writhed around through the night, Jill, the ever-vigilant nurse, suspected I was suffering from pancreatitis and ran me to Accident and Emergency at Selly Oak Hospital. She was dead right and, within half an hour, I was on a couple of drips and oxygen. Doctors told me I would have had it, if I had not reached hospital so quickly. Lucky for me that we lived in a city, not a remote outpost miles away in the mountains. We never knew exactly what caused the problem. There was no sign of a gallstone and I am not a big drinker, although the medics were looking in that direction. In the end, it was thought I had probably caught a virus. It was all fairly frightening and I lost a stone and a half in about ten days. I struggled back to work sooner than I should, but the BBC were keen for me to front Midlands Today during the G8 talks in Birmingham, with President Bill Clinton and other world leaders in town.

That particular summit focused world attention on the Midlands and perhaps opened a few eyes about the region's positive points. Although I am a born-and-bred southerner, I am a great admirer of the rather under-estimated counties within easy reach of Birmingham. There really are some outstandingly beautiful towns, villages and landscapes in Derbyshire, Gloucestershire, Herefordshire, Staffordshire, Shropshire, Warwickshire and Worcestershire. My particular passion is for the countryside of Shropshire, which played such a part in my childhood and that of my father. For me, some of the poems of A.E.Housman in A Shropshire Lad capture the atmosphere of that unfashionable county quite perfectly. Housman was born near Bromsgrove in Worcestershire, but he felt inspired as a young man by the distant views of Shropshire on his western horizon. He yearned for them when he started work as a clerk in an office in London. He missed the rural peace of home and the carefree days of youth and those feelings of nostalgia prompted my favourite lines in English literature, written in the final decade of the nineteenth century.

Into my heart, an air that kills
   From yon far country blows:
What are those blue remembered hills,
   What spires, what farms are those?

That is the land of lost content,
   I see it shining plain,
The happy highways where I went
   And cannot come again.

Housman was a Professor of Latin at Cambridge University when my father was studying classics there. Bertie wanted to hear him give a talk on the Roman poet Lucretius and turned up at the appointed time to see the great man for the first time. He had long admired his poetry, particularly because of the Shropshire connection. To his bitter disappointment, a notice on the door proclaimed that the renowned professor was indisposed and the lecture had been cancelled. Housman died the following week on April 30th 1936.

What Housman would have made of the literary and media world of today defies imagination. I have been in television now, either at local or national level, for more than a quarter of a century and, although there are some dire programmes and quite abysmal abuse of the English language, I do think there is some good stuff about as well. It is just harder to find because there are so many channels. Endless makeover shows and reality programmes bore me rigid, but some of the factual, documentary output hidden away, whether on terrestrial or satellite channels, can be compulsive viewing. Sitcoms are not what they were, in my opinion, but current-day satirical comedy and sketch shows are sometimes quite brilliant. Have I Got News For You has that rare quality of making me laugh out loud and continues to be hilarious week after week. It never palls.

Of course, sport on the box has been revolutionised over the past decade. Sky Television has delivered a deluge of live football and led the way in all-pervasive coverage, including the introduction of the interactive red button. Fair enough, they have paid huge money and they can dictate where they go and whom they interview. I should imagine the snubs of yesteryear are a thing of the past. I remember being told where to stuff my microphone by Ron Saunders at Aston Villa after waiting for hours in a draughty corridor and being ordered to 'f**k off out of it' by Brian Clough at Nottingham Forest. That sort of thing was par for the course for hapless reporters, but the massive amounts of money changing hands rightly ensures maximum access for the company paying. Similarly, Sky opened up new horizons for cricket fans and not to be able to watch the England team abroad nowadays is unthinkable. That, for me, has been the greatest plus from Sky Sports. My one regret about their football is that the staggering sums of money involved have widened the gap between the Premiership and the leagues below. The heightened glamourisation of the big clubs has detracted from the appeal of the smaller outfits. Youngsters growing up today can get their football fix almost nightly, wherever they live, and have no need to show the remotest interest in what may be their second division, local clubs. Even so, Sky do serve the lower leagues right down to the Conference and all credit to them for that, but it is still a concern that the base of our country's soccer pyramid is tottering on rocky footings at the moment.

You will have gathered that I love my football and cricket, but I have never missed working in sport. I spend a considerable amount of my life at sporting events, but always as a fan. As I said earlier, I found the working side of it rather restricting in the climate that prevailed with ITV in the eighties and nineties.

However, I still thoroughly enjoy my work in television, with no two days ever the same. It is relentless, five days a week for around 47 weeks a year, but every day throws up a new challenge in script writing, preparing a live interview, or the broadcast itself. I hope I never take it for granted.

I almost titled this book, It's a Privilege, because I am eternally grateful for the opportunities journalism, broadcasting and television, in particular, have given me. As you will have gathered, I have been lucky enough to interview Prime Ministers, rub shoulders with Royalty, and chat to major showbusiness stars from Charlton Heston to Bob Hope, from Arnold Schwarzenegger to Morecambe and Wise. In sport, I have been involved with giants of their generations, among them footballers Stanley Matthews, Billy Wright, Jimmy Greaves, Bobby Charlton, Denis Law plus George Best, Maradona and Pele. Cricketers including Gary Sobers, Viv Richards, Clive Lloyd, Ian Botham, Colin Cowdrey, Peter May and Basil D'Oliveira. Basil, of course, will go down as a pivotal figure in changing sporting history and contributing to the death of apartheid. I have felt honoured to meet brilliant medical pioneers who are driven by a mission to conquer fatal disease and improve our quality of life. I have felt humbled to meet so-called ordinary people and their families who have shown astonishing courage in coping with dreadful personal tragedy.

And while we are talking about courage, how humbling it is to meet the irrepressible survivors of World War Two concentration camps. To most of us, it is just impossible to conceive of their suffering. It was an enormous privilege to stand shoulder-to-shoulder with my father on his return to Dunkirk and, four years later, to visit the beaches of Normandy for the sixtieth anniversary of the D Day landings. We broadcast three live programmes from Arromanches, the focal point of the allied invasion, and mingled with the first men to drop behind enemy lines in the early hours of June 6th 1944. We now know that fateful day marked the beginning of the end of the war, but what must have been going through the minds of those young men as they drifted down in the darkness onto hostile territory? Every veteran, of whatever rank, whatever service, has an enthralling, if not fearsome, tale to tell. My colleagues Chris, Robin, Ian, Howard and I talked to the German sentry who was on duty at Pegasus Bridge when the first gliders landed. We chatted to Arlette Gondree-Pritchett, whose family home by the bridge was the first building to be liberated by the Allies. She was a young girl at the time, but I was struck by how grateful she felt to our troops – in fact, that seemed to be the case with all the French people we met in Normandy. I was constantly conscious of the awesome history of the place, but never more overwhelmed with it all than the moment I entered the cemetery at Ranville, not far from Pegasus. It was a truly beautiful and peaceful place, although the church itself was scarred with bullet holes from some fierce gun battles shortly after D Day. Hundreds of gleaming white graves stood row after row after row in a beautifully manicured setting. English flowers, English grass, English stone. Died June 6th, aged 22. Died June 7th, aged 24 and so on. Every one a life cut tragically short and you imagine the grief of the family back home on receiving the dreaded telegram. 'He answered the call in our darkest hour' was typical of the inscriptions. Amongst them all lies the grave of Lieutenant Den Brotheridge, the first serviceman to be killed by enemy action on D Day. He stormed out of the first glider to land in Normandy and perished under gunfire on Pegasus Bridge. I said on Midlands Today that those few days around Arromanches were some of the most memorable, emotional and evocative of my whole life and I certainly meant it. It was an immensely moving experience. A privilege to be there.

I also genuinely believe it is a privilege and a responsibility to be invited into people's homes via the television screen, as I am five days a week now in the Midlands. I still get keyed up too. Whatever the programme, I always become dry in the throat while the title music is playing and feel a surge in the pulse. They say that you would be unable to do the job properly without nerves. With experience, you learn how to cope, but the nerves never go away. A friend of mine once put it to me quite beautifully. "Butterflies are absolutely fine," she said. "The trick is getting them to fly in formation." Spot-on..... and I hope together the butterflies and I have plenty more flying hours ahead.

INDEX